WILD BORNEO

The wildlife and scenery of Sabah, Sarawak, Brunei and Kalimantan

Text *by* Nick Garbutt
Photography *by* Nick Garbutt *and* J. Cede Prudente

WWF *for a living planet*

Produced in association with WWF-Malaysia in
support of the Heart of Borneo Project

NEW HOLLAND

First published in 2006 by
New Holland Publishers (UK) Ltd
London • Cape Town • Sydney • Auckland

www.newhollandpublishers.com

Garfield House, 86–88 Edgware Road, London, W2 2EA,
United Kingdom
80 McKenzie Street, Cape Town 8001, South Africa
14 Acquatic Drive, Frenchs Forest, NSW 2086, Australia
218 Lake Road, Northcote, Auckland, New Zealand

ISBN 1 84537 378 2

Publishing Manager: Jo Hemmings
Senior Editor: Steffanie Brown
Design: Gülen Shevki-Taylor
Cartography: William Smuts
Production: Joan Woodroffe

Reproduction by Pica Digital Pte Ltd, Singapore
Printed and bound in Singapore by Star Standard Industries (Pte) Ltd

COVER AND PRELIMINARY PAGES:

Front Cover: Female Proboscis Monkey (*Nasalis larvatus*),
Kinabatangan River, Sabah

Back Cover: top: sunrise over lowland dipterocarp rainforest;
middle, left to right: *Rafflesia keithii* in bloom; Oriental Pied
Hornbill (*Anthracoceros albirostris*); Raja Brooke's Birdwing
(*Trogonoptera brookiana*)

Page 1: Keel-bellied Whip Snake (*Dryophiops rubescens*)

Page 2: Wrinkled Hornbill *(Aceros corrugatus)*

Page 4-5: Proboscis Monkey (*Nasalis larvatus*)

Page 6: Wagler's Pit Viper (*Tropidolaemus wagleri*) resting on a
Heliconia flower

Page 7: Pitcher Plant (*Nepenthes faizaliana*)

CONTENTS

PREFACE

Life on Earth is not evenly spread around our planet. Borneo – the world's third largest island – is one of its richest treasure-houses, full of an immense variety of wild animals and plants, all living in a magnificent tropical forest.

A single, vast, unbroken area of this forest still cloaks the mountains, foothills and adjacent lowlands that stretch along the inland borders of Brunei, Indonesia and Malaysia. This is the Heart of Borneo, and all of us who value life on this planet should support the efforts of these countries to conserve it. It is truly a world heritage and the world should respond to its needs.

Like almost all such forests, it is under the threat of being cleared or degraded, thanks to the economic and social pressures of life in the 21st century. We must not let this happen.

These forests are not just the home of wildlife. They protect the land and give birth to the island's rivers. They maintain a natural system that supports both the lives of the local people and their countries' economies.

Please join with me to help save the Heart of Borneo – a global heritage.

Sir David Attenborough

FOREWORD

For some of us, Borneo is simply home. For others, it is a far off land with a name that is redolent of headhunters, Orang-utans and steamy jungles. From any pespective, Borneo is one of the most important centres of biodiversity in the world. It teems with wildlife that is the envy of other places, yet we know for sure that there are still literally thousands of plants and animals still to be discovered. It is also home to the many indigenous cultures that the various Bornean peoples have developed in harmony with their natural environment.

WWF has spent decades working hand-in-hand with our many partners in conservation to help ensure a future for this extraordinary hothouse of nature. We have helped governments with research, with establishing parks and sanctuaries, and with managing the environment in a way that is sustainable. Of course, the frontiers of nature have fallen back under the pressure of modern development, and nobody should deny modern amenities and lifestyles to the people of this great island.

WWF believes that nature is best conserved when it meets the needs of people, without destroying the natural resources that support and enrich our lives in so many ways. Among those resources are the mighty forests that straddle the highland boundaries of Borneo's three countries: Brunei Darussalam, Indonesia and Malaysia. This is the Heart of Borneo – truly a green heart – which holds one of the last great bastions of Southeast Asian rainforest and gives birth to the rivers that are the arteries of the island. If nature conservation matters anywhere, it surely matters here.

This book is a celebration of one of the world's great treasure-troves of wildlife. Let it be a tribute to all who work together to save the heart and soul of Borneo.

Tengku Datuk Zainal Adlin
Vice-President Emeritus, WWF-Malaysia

INTRODUCTION

Few places conjure images of darkness and mystery like Borneo — the island has long nourished the imagination of naturalists and travellers alike. Charles Darwin once described it as 'one great wild untidy luxuriant hothouse made by nature for herself', an incredibly apt description, given the wealth and variety of fauna and flora on the island. There may not be the concentrations of easily seen animals that more glamorous wildlife locations, such as those in East Africa, have to offer, but this is more than compensated for by extraordinary species diversity and subtlety.

From the heights of Mount Kinabalu to pristine coral-fringed offshore islands with vast tracts of lush rainforest in between, the diversity of habitats supports a tremendous array of endearing and intriguing species – there are mammals, lizards, snakes and frogs that 'fly', fish that 'walk' on mud, monkeys that dive and swim, plants that eat insects and flowers the size of dustbin lids.

Borneo is a centre of biological richness for the Indo-Malayan region, and a hotspot of world biodiversity. Ten

BELOW LEFT: *This male Flying Lizard (*Draco cornutus*) is signalling to an opponent by flashing its triangular dewlap.*

BELOW RIGHT *The Oriental Pied Hornbill (*Anthracoceros albirostris*) is often seen in lowland areas around the forest edge.*

THE ISLAND OF BORNEO

Kinabalu
National Park

Mount
Kinabalu

Kota Kinabalu

Turtle Islands Marine Park

Sepilok Orang-utan
Sanctuary

Sandakan

Rafflesia Rainforest Reserve

SABAH

Kinabatangan
Wildlife Sanctuary

Tabin Wildlife Reserve

BRUNEI

Danum Valley
Conservation Area

Lahad Datu

Miri

Maliau Basin

Lambir Hills
National Park

Ulu Temberong
National Park

Gunung Mulu
National Park

SARAWAK

*EAST
KALIMANTAN*

Bako
National Park

Gunung Gading
National Park

Kuching

*WEST
KALIMANTAN*

*CENTRAL
KALIMANTAN*

Gunung Palung
Wildlife Reserve

Pangkalanbuun

Tanjung Puting
National Park

0   100   200   300 km

ABOVE: *Pitcher Plant (*Nepenthes rajah*); this is the largest species and perhaps the most famous of all pitcher plants. The huge pitchers are known to catch rats, frogs and lizards as well as insects.*

ABOVE: *The indigenous tribes of Borneo have lived in harmony with their environment for centuries and have used traditional methods to make blow pipes and hunt primates and other mammals.*

hectares (25 acres) of rainforest in Borneo can support a greater number of tree species than occur in the whole of North America. The island is home to more bird species than are found in Europe and as many mammals as live on the island continent of Australia.

Straddling the equator between 007° North and 004° South, and covering an area of nearly 740,000 square km (285,714 square miles), Borneo is the world's third largest island (after Greenland and New Guinea). It is divided politically between three countries: the states of Sarawak and Sabah are part of Malaysia and cover around 35 per cent; Kalimantan, which covers around 65 per cent of the island, belongs to Indonesia; and the small independent state of Brunei Darussaleam (normally abbreviated to Brunei) sandwiched between Sarawak and Sabah, covers less than 1 per cent.

Superficially, Borneo might seem rather flat, as large tracts – over 50 per cent – are lowland areas (less than 150m/490 feet

elevation) covered in rainforests and swamp forests (indeed only 6 per cent of the whole island is above 1000m/3300 feet elevation). Yet there are also significant mountain ranges that run through the island's interior from south-west to north-east. The centre of the island consists of the Iran Mountains and the Müller Mountains, from which several highland offshoots reach out to the west, south and east. Most of these upland areas do not exceed 2000m (6,600 feet) in altitude. At the north-western corner of the island is Borneo's summit, Mount Kinabalu; with its peak at 4095m (13,435 feet), it is the highest mountain in South-East Asia (between the Himalayas and New Guinea).

Rivers provide the main arteries of transport and communication from the island's interior to the coastal lowlands. The three longest rivers in Indonesia are in Kalimantan: the Kapuas at 1143km (710 miles) flows to the west coast, the Barito at 900km (560 miles) flows south, and the Mahakam at 775km (480 miles) disgorges into the

Sulawesi Sea on the east coast; while in Sabah the Kinabatangan River is born on the slopes of Trus Madi and the Maliau Basin and flows for 560km (350 miles) to the Sulu Sea. Most human settlements are concentrated along these and other major waterways and around the coasts.

The local climate is tropical equatorial, with temperatures ranging from 25°C (77°F) up to 35°C (95°F) in lowland areas. While heavy rain is a possibility every day of the year, and at least 200mm (8 inches) does fall most months, there is a marked 'wet' monsoon season between November and April and a 'dry' season from May until October.

Humans may first have arrived on the island more than 45,000 years ago, however, the ancestors of today's indigenous peoples (collectively often referred to as Dayaks) are thought to have settled around 4,500 years ago and initially colonized mainly the coastal lowlands, living as hunter-gatherers for centuries before turning towards agriculture, all the while maintaining a balanced sustainable relationship with their environment. It was only after the use of iron and other metals spread to Borneo that the indigenous peoples begin to exploit the rainforest environment and move into the interior. Today, the Dayaks are the island's farmers, and rice production and shifting cultivation have been germane to their culture. Since the emergence of monoculture cash crops and industrial logging, however, forest depletion and soil erosion have become serious areas of concern.

The first Europeans arrived in the early 16th century: in 1521, Pigafetta landed on the shores of Brunei Bay, and over the following 300 years numerous trading posts were established by Europeans along Borneo's north-western coasts. By 1526, a regular trade between Brunei and Portugal had

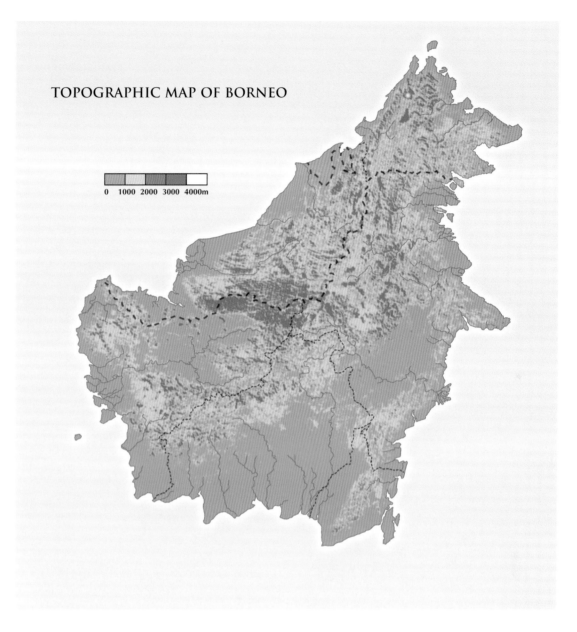

TOPOGRAPHIC MAP OF BORNEO

0   1000 2000 3000 4000m

developed, and it is from these early contacts the island as a whole became known as Borneo, apparently as a corruption of Brunei. Some of the earliest biological cataloguing was done by Alfred Russel Wallace, the British Victorian naturalist who happened on the theories of evolution at the same time as Charles Darwin (see Alfred Russel Wallace, page 15) – even though some of his first descriptions did not suggest great enthusiasm: in 1855 he wrote (of Sarawak in Borneo), 'As far inland as I have yet seen, this country may be briefly described as dead level, a dense forest and a perfect swamp. It would therefore be very uninviting, were it not for a few small hills which, here and there, rise abruptly – oases in the swampy wilderness.' However, he did show more enthusiasm for some of the wildlife, saying, 'One of the principal reasons that induced me to come here was that it is the country of those most strange and interesting animals, the Orang-utans.'

Development versus Conservation

Early exploration and development paved the way for the beginnings of the exploitation of the island's natural resources, and in the modern era, with the establishment of global markets, this exploitation has escalated substantially. In the mid-1980s about 75 per cent of Borneo's natural forest cover remained; today the figure is around 50 per cent, and destruction continues at an unnerving pace. On average, 850,000 hectares (2,100,350 acres) are lost every year.

This loss is not only the result of direct felling by logging operations, but also by forest fires caused by the changes deforestation brings. When pristine, rainforests are continually humid and largely immune to fire, even during unusually dry periods. After major felling, and slash-and-burn agriculture, tangled secondary forest replaces the rainforest and it is far more prone to drying out. In times of drought it burns easily and spreads over vast areas. In the past decade there have been massive fires affecting many parts of Kalimantan, and more than 5 million hectares has been lost.

Further, during the 1990's, the Suharto government (of Indonesia) allowed large areas of peat swamp forest in Kalimantan to be drained for agriculture, causing the underlying peat to dry out and become a tinderbox. Once alight, fires in these areas are all but impossible to extinguish. With such massive areas burning on a regular basis, there has been a colossal increase in the amount of carbon released in to the atmosphere. The detrimental effects this has had on the climate of the region and globally is impossible to quantify.

Trying to conserve the remaining biodiversity is therefore imperative, and presents a stern challenge not only to the conservation community, but also to the world as a whole. In Borneo, efforts to maintain biodiversity operate at many levels, from organizations fighting illegal logging and wildlife trade, to the welfare of orphaned Orang-utans, to broader holistic initiatives addressing ecosystems and habitats. Perhaps the greatest threats come from wholesale felling and destruction of forest areas, firstly for the timber, and secondly to convert to palm oil plantations. While no one can deny the various governments in Borneo the right to exploit their natural resources, it must be remembered that they are doing so largely to supply overseas markets.

In recent years, oil palm has been the major plantation crop to expand at the expense of forest. Major demand for palm oil comes from China, India, Europe and America. Markets, especially in the more 'environmentally-aware' West, can play a role in moderating the expansion of plantations into biologically significant forests and environmentally sensitive areas by requiring evidence that producer companies are acting responsibly. This trend is already underway through the international Roundtable on Sustainable Palm Oil.

At the forefront of contemporary initiatives is the *Heart of Borneo* concept, a large-scale and challenging proposal whereby the three governments of Borneo will work in concert with the conservation community to preserve the core highland areas and peripheral biodiversity-rich lowlands that are the lifeblood of the island. Few who read this book would deny that a world without Orang-utans, Proboscis Monkeys, Rhinoceros Hornbills and *Rafflesias* would be a sorry place. Moreover, without the forests these species inhabit, Borneo would diminish to a barren wasteland, incapable of providing a home for its people. Retention of a series of protected forest areas, along with well-managed timber-production forests in the Heart of Borneo, would help to prevent this. This initiative must succeed, not only for the good of Borneo, but also for the world as a whole.

LEFT: *Large-scale timber extraction, largely to supply markets in the West, India, China and Japan, is a major threat to the remaining rainforests.*

ALFRED RUSSEL WALLACE

Alfred Russel Wallace is perhaps best known for having developed the theory of evolution by natural selection at the same time as Charles Darwin, though he allowed Darwin to take all the plaudits. However, his contribution to biology, and in particular to ideas of species distribution in South-East Asia, is immense. He is effectively the founding father of the theories of biogeography.

Between 1854 and 1862, Wallace travelled widely around the Indonesian Archipelago, shipping home skins of birds, various mammals, butterflies, beetles, numerous plants and much more besides. In all, his collections amounted to a staggering 127,000 specimens, but it is for his thoughts and theories on two questions that he is remembered.

Firstly, like Darwin he was fascinated by where species came from. Others had tentatively suggested that species were not immutable and could change with time, but no one knew how this might work. Wallace and Darwin were thinking deeply on the subject around the same time (and indeed corresponded), but Darwin's thoughts had stagnated. Then in 1858, while Alfred Wallace was in the Moluccas Islands, the penny dropped and he had his moment of great insight, and quickly penned an article entitled 'On the Tendency of Varieties to Depart Indefinitely from the Original Type'. Succinctly and with clarity, Wallace had arrived at much the same conclusions to do with a subject that Darwin had been pondering for years. There were differences: Darwin argued that it was competition between individuals that resulted in the 'survival of the fittest', whereas Wallace considered that individuals were in competition with their environment, and those that survived were the ones who best fitted into it. Nonetheless, Darwin and Wallace joined forces to present their theories jointly to the scientific world in a paper to the Linnean Society in London in 1858. Neither man attended.

Alfred Wallace's second remarkable insight concerned the distribution of species in South-East Asia. Wallace travelled more thoroughly around the region than anyone previously, and gained insight into which species occurred where. He noticed a very clear divide running through the islands, commenting, 'one half shall truly belong to Asia, and the other shall no less certainly be allied to Australia.' This line separated the islands of Bali and Lombok, only 25km (15.5 miles) apart: the birds in Bali were definitely of Asian stock, yet Lombok was home to species similar to those in Australia. The line continued north, and to its west on Borneo were monkeys, cats and elephants, yet to the line's east on islands such as Celebes (now Sulawesi) and New Guinea, these forms were absent and replaced with marsupials and other unmistakably Australian forms.

Wallace had effectively discovered the boundary of two continental plates that were converging. Millions of years before, the islands and their inhabitants would have been far apart, but continental drift had subsequently brought them together to such intimate juxtaposition. This fault line still exists and is known as Wallace's Line, and it separates two of the planet's great zoogeographical regions, the Oriental and the Australian.

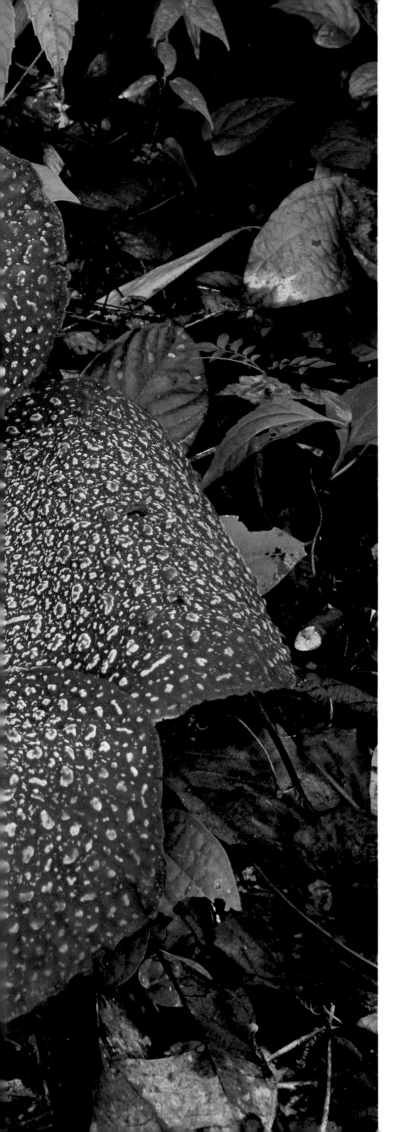

THE HABITATS & FLORA OF BORNEO

Borneo may well have the greatest plant diversity of any region on earth. Conservative estimates suggest that Borneo contains more than 15,000 plant species, including over 3,000 species of tree, in excess of 2,500 orchids and more than 50 carnivorous pitcher plants. A high proportion of the island's plants are endemic: a figure in excess of 6,000 has been suggested, including 155 endemic species of dipterocarp tree, which effectively form the towering scaffolding around which the intricate ecological web of a lowland rainforest is constructed. While lowland forests dominate the island's habitats, other important and diverse floral communities create unique habitats that are vital components in Borneo's biodiversity. This variation is created by three factors: proximity to the coast and the influence of salinity; drainage patterns and susceptibility to periodic flooding; and increase in altitude. Other factors influencing plant communities are soil type, slope and aspect; in many cases, variations in these factors produce subtle changes in micro-habitat. Nonetheless, five major floral communities can be recognized.

MANGROVE AND NIPA COASTAL FOREST

Mangroves dominate the intermediate zone between land and sea. While the ebb and flow of the tides presents serious survival difficulties, it also provides a rich and regular influx of nutrients which some specialized and a handful of adaptable plant and animal species have evolved to exploit.

The boundary zone between terrestrial and marine environments is both crucial and harsh. It is crucial in that it acts as a buffer that cushions the land from the sea, and it is harsh because of the constant changes in salinity. Yet the species that have been able to adapt to these demands have colonized an environment rich in resources and opportunity.

PREVIOUS PAGE: *Rafflesia in bloom;* Rafflesia keithii *is the largest species found in Borneo; blooms may reach over 90cm (35 inches) in diameter.*

OPPOSITE: *Long-tailed Macaques (*Macaca fascicularis*) often venture into mangrove areas to forage for fruits, or to sift through fresh detritus on the mud flats brought in by the previous tide.*

BELOW: *Mangrove swamps are an intricate maze of shifting sediments, water channels and trees.*

Mangrove Forest

Throughout the tropical areas of the world it is mangroves that dominate this intermediate zone. Mangroves themselves are a diverse group that have evolved some remarkable adaptations to cope with the rigours their environment imposes: firstly, they are tolerant of the high salinity; and secondly, they are able to deal with lack of oxygen and aeration caused by the thick sandy mud in which they grow, and the twice-a-day inundation of the tides. One of the overriding first impressions of mangroves at low tide is the mass of twig-like sticks growing like a forest of miniature spears all around the bases of the larger trees. These are actually roots that have grown up to protrude above the mud surface, through which the mangrove is able to absorb not only oxygen from the air, but nutrients from the water.

The major root systems of mangroves are a tangle of arches that, as they become established, form a barrier between the

sea and the land. Silt is constantly deposited by sediment-laden rivers flowing into estuaries, but is then moved and shifted by the changing tides and the sea. As mangroves develop, silt deposits collect and stabilize around their roots and provide new opportunities for seedlings to colonize. With further increases in the size of the mangroves, more and more silt collects around their roots until it becomes new land. Therefore mangroves comprise an ever-changing environment, where water courses alter, silt is eroded and sediments are deposited.

While the ebb and flow of the tides presents survival difficulties to be overcome, it also presents opportunity, as there is a regular and reliable influx of nutrients for the trees and the animal communities around them to exploit. It is no surprise then that mangroves are productive environments with high growth rates. Nutrients brought in on the tides are supplemented by leaves and fruits falling from the trees on to the mud below, and this bounty is tapped by all manner of fauna, from micro-organisms to crabs, prawns, molluscs, fish and even some primates. Indeed, the plentiful food supply and the sanctuary offered by the tangle of roots makes mangroves vital nurseries for the juvenile stages of many crustaceans and fish.

While the productivity and importance of mangroves in the overall marine web has now been realized, their economic

ABOVE: *Spectacular formations of aerial roots are one of the hallmarks of mangroves.*

potential has been quick to be exploited. Major fishing communities are often to be found close to areas of mangroves, and now their potential for prawn farming is being developed. However, caution must be exercised, as too many prawn farms in certain areas has dramatically altered the balance within inter-tidal zones, to the detriment of other species.

Mudskippers

Some of the most unusual inhabitants of mangrove areas are mudskippers, a rather unique group of fish belonging to the goby family (family Gobiidae, subfamily Oxudercinae). There are actually numerous different species that all exploit silt and mudflats around mangroves and nipa palm forest. During high tides they live in water much the same as any other small coastal fish, but as the tide recedes, they become evident, climbing out on to the roots of mangroves and exposed areas of mud. Out of water, mudskippers become more like an amphibian than a fish, filling their gill chambers with a mixture of air and water to breath, and grazing over the surface of the muddy ooze for newly deposited nutrients.

TOP: *Mudskippers are amongst the few species of fish that have evolved techniques that allow them to breath out of water. They are commonly seen on exposed mud near estuaries and mangroves.*

BOTTOM: *Outside their burrows, male Fiddler Crabs signal to their neighbours as a territorial defence.*

RIGHT: *The Ruddy Kingfisher (Halcyon coromanda) is a rare inhabitant of coastal forest areas and hunts primarily in estuaries and the sea.*

Coastal areas by their very nature represent a zone of transition – they are where the marine environment meets the terrestrial environment – yet there is very little traffic between the two. Species are generally adapted to exploit either one or the other, but rarely both. Of course some terrestrial species, like many sea birds, make feeding forays into the sea, but in all other ways the birds are tied to the land. Conversely, some marine species, like turtles, are forced to return to land very briefly to reproduce. Mudskippers are amongst the very small number of specialists who have found a way to straddle the two biomes, and quite literally exploit the best of both worlds.

These fish are found on mudflats around tropical coasts in West Africa, the Indian Ocean, South-East Asia and parts of the western Pacific. Worldwide there are around 40 species, many of which occur around the coasts of Borneo, wherever there are mangroves and mudflats.

As the waters begin to recede after a high tide, areas of mud become exposed, and anyone looking closely will begin to see these small fish – they average around 10cm (4 inches) in length, although the largest species reach more than 25cm (10 inches) – hauling themselves out of their 'natural' environment into the apparently 'alien' world of land and air. They have modified pectoral fins that are used in tandem, like a pair of crutches; their eyes are like periscopes and sit on top of their heads (so they can see above water even when their bodies are partially submerged), and to keep the eyes moist when out of water, the fish can rotate them downwards into liquid retained at the bottom of the socket.

So baffled were early travellers by the mudskipper's terrestrial forays that they concluded that the fish somehow breathed through its tail by keeping it immersed while lolling on shore. Obviously the truth is rather different. By necessity, a fish that spends half of its life out of water requires specialized breathing apparatus. When under water, a mudskipper breathes like any other fish, drawing water in through the mouth and passing it across gill filaments that

remove dissolved oxygen. But without the support of water, regular fish cannot keep their gills operational out of water: the gills collapse and dry out, and ultimately the fish suffocates. To counteract this, mudskippers fill their gill chambers with a mixture of air and water when they initially emerge. This portable life-support system, a sort of 'Aqua-lung' in reverse, maintains the gill structure and keeps it moist, so it continues to function during the mudskipper's time on land. With leg-like pectoral fins and the ability to breath out of water, it is easy to envisage that mudskippers must in some way resemble the ancestors of the first creatures that crawled out of the sea to colonize the land.

Once out of water, the mudskippers graze the surface of the sediment for fresh algae deposited by the latest tide. Larger species are more predatory and feed on small crustaceans and molluscs. They are highly territorial, defending an area around a burrow that they reside in when the tide is up. At low tide, males in particular can be highly aggressive towards intruders, posturing, mouth-gaping and signalling with an erect dorsal fin.

Mudskippers show a surprising degree of parental care. For instance, Giant Mudskippers (*Periophthalmodon schlosseri*) excavate a deep nest burrow with their mouth, as much as 1.2m (4 feet) long. A low wall is built around the entrance, so there is always a pool of water over the entrance at low tide. Sometimes several entrances are built. The eggs are laid on the roof of a chamber at the rear of the burrow, where there is little oxygen. To overcome this problem, the parents gulp mouthfuls of air, take it into the burrow, and release it around the eggs. After hatching, the larvae initially remain in the burrow; when more mature they spend time in the safety of the pool around the nest entrance.

Nipa Forest

Further inland from the inter-tidal zone, the influence of the sea is literally diluted by fresh water flowing from the interior. In these areas, mangroves give way to nipa palms, which form dense monoculture stands that flank the lower reaches of many of Borneo's larger rivers. Nipa forests are extremely thick and impenetrable, and offer limited potential for exploitation by other species. Their buds are high in sugars, and are eaten by both Long-tailed Macaques and Proboscis Monkeys that venture into the forests from time to time. In some areas, the nipa fronds are harvested by local people for thatch, which is dried and used as roofing, to construct walls and to make matting.

LEFT: *In low-lying coastal regions and estuaries, where regular flooding occurs, dense stands of mangroves and nipa palms dominate and form an almost impenetrable barrier.*

FRESHWATER SWAMP FOREST

There are two varieties of swamp forest: one type flourishes on alluvial soils, the fertility of which encourages tall, diverse forest that is rich in wildlife; the other grows on acidic soils, and is relatively infertile. Exploitation of both types has had far-reaching detrimental effects on both ecology and climate.

In coastal lowland areas, elevation often rises only very gradually away from the sea, and the influence of the tides can reach upriver and far inland. However, where the salinity ceases to have an effect, a dramatically different forest is able to grow, one no longer flooded by the sea, but instead one that is regularly subjected to floods when rivers overflow after heavy rain. This is freshwater swamp forest.

Riverine Forest

There are two distinct varieties of swamp forest, depending on the substrate on which they grow. One type flourishes on nutrient-rich alluvial soils that are deposited by major rivers,

the fertility of the soil allowing the growth of tall diverse forest with high leaf and fruit productivity that is correspondingly rich in wildlife. Next to rivers, the swamp soils are elevated due to frequent deposition of silt, while away from rivers the

OPPOSITE: *Remaining freshwater swamp and riverine forest is one of the strongholds of the Bornean Pygmy Elephant (*Elephas maximus 'borneensis'*).*

BELOW: *The morning sun breaks through along the banks of the Menanggol River, a tributary of the Kinabatangan River in Sabah.*

LEFT: *Oriental Darters (*Anhinga melanogaster*) lack preen glands; they must dry their feathers or they'll become waterlogged.*

BELOW: *One characteristic of swamp forest is that it regularly floods, bringing a regular supply of nutrients to the forest.*

subject to extensive conversion to agriculture throughout Asia, particularly rice and, in Borneo, oil palm plantations. Unchecked this has had a severely detrimental effect on the ecology of areas such as the Lower Kinabatangan.

Peat Swamp Forest

In contrast, the soil is relatively infertile within swamp forest that grows on acidic soils composed of decaying plant material. Commonly known as peat swamp forest, this forest dominates areas in Sarawak and parts of southern Kalimantan. Although unsuitable for all crops except pineapple and oil palms, these forests do produce much sought-after hardwoods, and so they have been heavily exploited in places. The detrimental effects of this exploitation are far-reaching, as these forests play a crucial role in absorbing precipitation, and later releasing it slowly to the wider environment. With the forest removed, this 'sponge' effect is severely compromised.

land tends to be lower and permanently waterlogged, with different associations of tree species. The forests in the floodplain of the lower Kinabatangan river in east Sabah are one of the best examples, and harbour some of the largest remaining populations of wild Orang-utans, Proboscis Monkeys and Bornean Pygmy Elephants, as well as a wonderful diversity of birds, reptiles and amphibians.

Because of the soil fertility, these alluvial areas have been

DIPTEROCARP FOREST

Borneo's rainforests are the tallest on earth, and have the greatest diversity of plant and animal species; they also harbour more flying and gliding animals than any other forest. Trees are slow-growing and extremely old. Tropical rainforests throughout South-East Asia, including Borneo, are dominated by one family of trees, Dipterocarpaceae, from which the type takes its name; it is probably the most important wildlife habitat on earth.

Most tropical rainforests in the lowlands throughout South-East Asia, including Borneo, are dominated by one family of trees, Dipterocarpaceae, from which the forest type takes it name. This name itself (from the Greek) describes the seeds that many species produce: *di* = two, *ptero* = wing, and *carp* = seed. However, many members of the family have seeds with more than two wings (some have three or five, or even none), but they nonetheless share a mutually-supportive survival mechanism. So many seeds are produced at once, by so many species, that not all can be destroyed by fungi, bacteria, insects and mammals.

The diptocarp forest is the dominant climax habitat on Borneo. It dominates all areas below 900m (3,000 feet) elevations that do not flood on a regular basis. In its pristine state perhaps more than 80 per cent of the island was covered in this forest type.

Dipterocarp forest is *the* classical rainforest and epitomizes the popular notion of a *jungle*. However, 'jungle' is a misnomer that has become entrenched in common parlance: in actual fact the term is derived from the Hindi word *'jangal'*, meaning waste ground, and was coined in eighteenth-century India to describe the 'wild, impenetrable tangle of vegetation' that grew on waste areas. So for the sake of accuracy, 'tropical lowland rainforest' is a better encompassing description.

Although our perception may be that rainforests are a confused tangle of impenetrable vegetation, nothing could actually be further from the truth. Dense, tangled undergrowth is mainly found at the boundaries, along river banks, or where there are clearings created by fallen trees: all of these correspond to places where light is able to penetrate. The interior of untouched rainforest is dark, so little is able to

RIGHT: *After a damp night in Danum Valley, mist hangs above a river; the morning sun will eventually burn it off and the view will be clear.*

establish itself at lower levels; thus, far from the interior being a tangled mass, it is in places quite open and inviting. The hub of the rainforest is therefore not at ground level at all, it is way up in the canopy, where the impact of the warming sun and quenching rain are at their maximum.

Until relatively recently, the forest canopy was unknown; now, however, technology allows scientists to climb up and work in this 'high frontier'. What they are beginning to realize is that diptocarp forest is probably the most biologically diverse habitat on earth: some have estimated that half of all the species that exist may live in the rainforest canopies of the world – and it is likely that the canopies of Borneo are at the forefront of this diversity.

Major fruiting of dipterocarp trees rarely occurs in

successive years; instead the interval is irregular and may be over a decade. Then, for some reason the majority of mature trees of nearly all the dipterocarp species in the area will flower in the same season. The trigger for this synchronization is linked to a dry period and drop in temperature following a prolonged wet season.

Typically the main canopy of dipterocarp forest is usually 25-45m (80-150 feet) high, with many trees – the so-called emergents – reaching far beyond this to heights of around 60m (200 feet) or more. These are the tallest tropical rainforests on earth and are home to the greatest diversity of plant and animal species. Some of the dominant dipterocarp species include members of the genera *Shorea, Dipterocarpus, Parashorea, Drybalanops* and *Hopea*.

Although dipterocarps dominate the forest in appearance and represent the single family with the greatest number of trees, they do not dominate overall: indeed, the majority of trees in the forest are not members of the family, and this includes some of the tallest tree species. The Menggaris, or Tapang, (*Koompassia excelsa*) is actually a member of the bean family (Fabaceae) and regularly exceeds 60m (200 feet) in height, with some individuals reaching nearly 90m (300 feet), with trunk diameters approaching 3m (10 feet). The Menggaris is not only recognizable by its immense size, but also by its straight cylindrical trunk and pale grey bark. Giant Honey Bees (*Apis dorsata*) often build their huge half-moon comb nests beneath the horizontal branches of a Menggaris; this often means indigenous peoples are reluctant to fell them, as they instead prefer to maintain a regular and reliable source of honey. However, collection from such monumental trees is both difficult and dangerous and involves skilled climbers; it is usually attempted after dark, when the bees are less active. In some forests, over 90 per cent of bees' nests are curiously in Menggaris trees. This may partly be because, being so tall, they are difficult, if not impossible, for Sun Bears to climb; elsewhere these bears are major honey predators. But a key factor is that bees can navigate and find their way back most easily to the tallest emergent trees.

Trees in tropical forests are very slow-growing, a fact that seems somewhat paradoxical given that the warm wet conditions are ideal for plant growth. But from the outset, the odds against a seed developing

LEFT: *One of the tallest and most distinctive trees in the forest is the stately Menggaris (*Koompassia excelsa*), which regularly protrudes above the canopy.*

into a mature tree are incredibly small: from its first days after germination it faces a constant battle. Initially, this is to find enough light to photosynthesize and grow. Alfred Wallace once described the rainforests of Borneo as 'exceedingly gloomy and monotonous', the reason being that the canopy above is exceedingly dense – perhaps only 2 per cent of light falling on top of the canopy itself actually reaches the forest floor below – and new seedlings are in constant competition with other seedlings to snare what light there is. Constant low light inhibits rapid growth.

Where a gap suddenly appears in the canopy – say, if a mature tree is blown down in a storm – there is a dramatic rush from all saplings to reach the light. Under such circumstances they grow very quickly straight up with few leaves, desperate to reach their goal ahead of the competition. Should they succeed, the seedling then produces leaves very quickly in an attempt to plug the gap in the canopy, cut off the light, and effectively starve any competing saplings below. From this point, growth is outwards, rather than upwards.

Rainforests are also full of other species, hell-bent on making a meal of plants, whether it is primates or insects eating the leaves or fungi, and micro-organisms attacking their interior. To combat this, the trees have evolved various defences, and Dipterocarps produce indigestible fibres and chemicals such as tannins that bind to protein and prevent absorption in the gut. The majority of other plants also manufacture chemicals and toxins primarily to prevent leaf predators consuming too much in one sitting. But the manufacture and maintenance of such defences is a significant drain on the resources of a tree, and diverts energy away from simply growing.

Another factor in their slow growth is that they actually grow on nutrient-deficient soils. These soils are also very thin, so rather than roots penetrating downwards, they instead grow outwards and form an intricate latticework across the forest floor. For stability and support, trees then develop buttress roots, and on the largest trees these can reach colossal proportions.

The flipside to slow growth is longevity, and trees in Borneo's lowland rainforests, particularly the large ones, may be extremely old. For instance, the Bornean Ironwood (*Eusideroxylon zwageri*), locally known as Belian or Ulin, is one of the world's hardest and densest woods. Not only do the trees live for several hundred years, they also take a similar period of time to decay after their death.

A number of trees that grow in the forest understorey produce their flowers and fruits directly on their trunks. This is called 'cauliflory', and one possible reason for this is the stillness of the air below the forest canopy. Without air movement, trees beneath the canopy need to find an

TOP: *The Maiden's Veil Fungus (*Dictyphora duplicata*) is a common but rarely seen species in lowland forests.*

BOTTOM: *The falling seed of a giant Dipterocarp tree quickly descends to the forest floor, twirling around like a miniature helicopter.*

alternative means of dispersing their seeds. By producing succulent fruits, these trees entice a variety of fruit-eating animals – such as primates, small mammals, some birds and many insects – to lower levels in the forest. Once the fruits have been eaten, the seeds are dispersed far and wide in the animals' droppings.

The Flying Animals of the Forest

The forests of Borneo are perhaps the richest and certainly the tallest rainforests on earth. They also harbour a greater diversity of flying and gliding animals than any other forests. Not only are there the expected birds and bats, there are also flying squirrels, flying frogs, flying snakes, flying lizards, flying geckos and the bizarre Colugo or Flying Lemur. Why should this be?

Superficially, Borneo's rainforests appear very similar to the other great rainforests of the world: those of equatorial West Africa and the Amazon Basin in South America. Yet, the African forests have only a few flying squirrels or Anomalures (*Family Anomaluridae*), and no examples from other animal groups, while the mighty Amazon boasts no examples of 'flying' animals at all (other than the obvious bats and birds).

Is it simply a coincidence, a quirk of evolutionary fate that all these different groups in Borneo have hit upon 'flight' as a means of getting around, or is there more to it than meets the eye? Evolution rarely leaves anything to chance: if something has evolved, whether physical or behavioural, it is usually for good reason. And that invariably means that it in some way conveys an advantage to the individual.

Recent advances in technology have allowed scientists to begin exploring the rainforest canopy – considered by many the last great frontier on land – for the first time. These studies have not only focused on the species living in the canopy, but also on the structure of the canopy and the forest itself. From such lofty vantages, perspectives change dramatically. Comparisons, between the forests of Africa and the Amazon and those in Borneo (and other parts of South-East Asia) have revealed some surprising differences. While those in Africa and the Amazon show a degree of uniformity, with a closed canopy at a consistent height, those in Borneo appear more random, with no discernable uniform canopy height, and the presence of a large number of trees protruding way above the canopy (so-called emergents). Further, the rainforests of Africa and the New World are criss-crossed with vines and lianas that are far less evident in Borneo.

These differences obviously have profound implications for the way animals get around. In the closed canopies of Africa and the Amazon, the intricate network of inter-linking branches and vines creates a myriad of continuous highways

OPPOSITE: *A Flying Lizard (Draco sp.) launches itself from a tree trunk and glides effortlessly across a large gap in the forest. Using its tail, the lizard is able to 'steer' in mid air and control the direction of its 'flight'.*

ABOVE: *The Colugo, or Flying Lemur (Cynocephalus variegates), has unusual membranes between its limbs that form 'wings' (called a patagium), and is able to glide prodigious distances, even at night.*

RIGHT: *Several species of frog have also evolved the ability to 'glide' using the webbing on their feet as parachutes. One such species is the Harlequin Flying Frog (Rhacophorus pardalis).*

through the tree tops. With few or no breaks along the way, this allows animals to move around with complete freedom, never needing to descend to lower levels. In Borneo, this is not the case as the canopy is broken and the forest has many more layers or strata, from the tops of the tallest emergents to the main canopy, the sub-canopy and the understorey. There are, therefore, no continuous highways through the tree tops, and without these, animals would need to descend one tree, scamper across lower branches or the ground and then ascend a neighbouring tree to continue their arboreal journey. Obviously, this would be inefficient, tedious and potentially hazardous, as it would increase their vulnerability to predators.

Evolving the ability to 'fly' solves this problem perfectly; if there is no way to walk across, just climb up and jump across the gap in the forest. Even today, it is easy to observe how this trend might have begun: the non-flying squirrels of Borneo are superb climbers and acrobats and are able to leap easily between branches. Prevost's Squirrel, for instance, is a moderate-sized species, but is more than capable of jumping across gaps of several metres. If way back in squirrel evolution a similar species did the same, but just by chance developed

LEFT: *Many trees in lowland forest, such as this fig tree (Ficus sp.), flower and fruit directly from their trunks. This is known as 'cauliflory'.*

OPPOSITE TOP: *Borneo's dipterocarp forest canopy is perhaps the most biologically diverse habitat on earth.*

OPPOSITE BOTTOM: *The canopy of rainforest in Borneo does not form a 'closed' surface at a uniform height.*

small flaps of skin on its limbs, these might allow it to leap just that little bit further and gain advantage over others in the population. If the ability to grow flaps of skin was passed on to its offspring, then this trait would spread through the population and expand, as those with slightly bigger flaps of skin would always have the edge. It doesn't take a leap of faith to see how this trend leads to the evolution of flying squirrels.

Of course, the term 'flying' that is applied to all the different groups in Borneo is not strictly accurate: bats and birds are the only vertebrates with true powered flight. The majority would be much better described as 'gliders', as they are able to traverse large gaps and cover considerable distances in the air, but always constrained by gravity: they leap from high and land lower down. The Colugo or Flying Lemur, the flying squirrels and the flying lizards (*Draco* sp.) are the prime examples of this. Flying geckos, flying frogs and flying snakes are somewhat less sophisticated; their mode of aviation would be better described as a controlled fall or 'parachute'. All species have flaps of skin or other methods of dramatically increasing their surface area, to provide air resistance. This slows their descent, and also allows horizontal movement during the fall, with a degree of control and manoeuvrability.

TOP: *Kuhl's Gliding Gecko (*Ptychozoon kuhli), *found in many lowland forest areas, such as Danum Valley, uses flaps of skin on its legs, tails and body as 'parachutes' during its glides.*

LEFT: *While not a 'flying' species, Prevost's Squirrel (*Callosciurus prevostii) *is capable of spectacular leaps across gaps in the canopy.*

ABOVE: *Wallace's Flying Frog (*Rhacophorus nigropalmatus) *is considered the original 'Flying Frog of Borneo'. While it is primarily a canopy resident, this species descends to the forest floor to lay its eggs in foam nests above seasonal turbid pools.*

HEATH FOREST

Tropical heath forest develops in sandy soils, and plants that flourish in it have specifically adapted to the lack of nutrients; they are therefore rarely found elsewhere. For example, ant plants, and in particular the carnivorous pitcher plants, are typical, and Borneo has a greater diversity of species than any other locality.

Tropical heath forest develops on acidic, leached sandy soils that are very deficient in nutrients. In Borneo these forests are often referred to as '*kerangas*', a word derived from Iban dialect aptly meaning '*forested land, which, if cleared, will not grow rice*'. The forest is not constrained by altitude, and on pristine Borneo, heath forest grew on sandy soil in many coastal areas, particularly in the west, as well as montane areas with similar soils. Today, many of the coastal examples have disappeared, although there are still stands of heath forest on the coast in Bako National Park and other west coast areas in Sarawak. Montane examples of heath forest are more widespread, as many remain in isolated areas in the interior of the island – for instance the ridge tops of the Maliau Basin in Sabah.

In comparison with dipterocarp forest, heath forest is characterized by its lower canopy, generally 7 to 20m (23 to 65 feet), and dense stands of smaller sized, smaller crowned trees that often have small leaves. The canopy cover is also more uniform, with no emergent trees.

Plants that flourish in heath forests have specifically adapted to the lack of nutrients and are, therefore, rarely found elsewhere. With nutrients in such short supply, it is imperative that plants protect what they do manage to accumulate; many species in heath forest therefore contain very high concentrations of tannins and other poisons in their leaves to prevent excessive browsing by a range of herbivores.

In montane heath forests, the soil normally incorporates a substantial layer of peat close to the surface. This peat develops because of the very slow breakdown to organic mulch of the tannin-rich leaf litter. In turn, this reduced decomposition is a consequence of low temperatures at higher altitudes, waterlogging, and because there are so few invertebrates, such as termites. Effectively, this means the quantity of nutrients released into the soil is drastically reduced, and as a result, a number of plants have evolved extra nutrient-gathering techniques to supplement the meagre

RIGHT: *Typical heath forest growing from nutrient deficient soils.*

rations on offer from the soil.

Examples are the so-called ant plants, of which there are numerous species. All of them are easily recognizable by their large, bulbous grey tubers that grow attached to the trunks of trees. In most species the tubers are around 15 to 20cm (6 to 8 inches) in diameter, but in larger species they may reach the size of a football. Those belonging to the genus *Myrmecodia* (its literal meaning being 'ant house') are typical: their stem bases form swollen, spine-covered tubers that are compart-

Pitcher Plants

An alternative approach to getting extra nutrients is demonstrated by the pitcher plants (genus *Nepenthes*) that are a feature of both heath forest areas and some higher elevation montane areas in Borneo. These remarkable plants have evolved highly modified leaves that form 'bucket traps' for insects. The structures are intricate and vary between species, but the principal essentially remains the same. Insects are attracted into the pitcher, where they fall into the liquid at the bottom, drown and then gradually decompose. The plant then absorbs the released nutrients directly. Common heath forest pitcher plants include *Nepenthes gracilis*, *N. ampullaria* and *N. albomarginata*, while *N. bicalcarata* and *N. veitchii* are less common. The latter species is common in the Maliau Basin.

Although true pitcher plants (genus *Nepenthes*) are widely distributed through South-East Asia and some outlying localities as far west as Madagascar and east to New Caledonia, few would deny that Borneo boasts a diversity of species more spectacular than anywhere else. They are a conspicuous and integral part of the island's flora that have become synonymous with it. (*Nepenthes* is derived from the Greek meaning, 'removing all sorrow'. It is thought to refer to the drug opium that was later fancifully applied to the liquid inside a pitcher. The notion was seized upon by Linneaus, who adopted it as the generic name).

While it may not be unique in the botanical world, the concept of a plant catching and feeding on animals is a compelling one. Add to this their distinctiveness, unusual habits, beauty and in some instances, accessibility, and it is easy to see why interest in pitcher plants is high. The pitchers of some species hang individually above ground level, while others grow as clusters on the forest floor. Indeed there are instances where some species produce both aerial pitchers and terrestrial pitchers; for example, *N. bicalcarata*.

The pitchers themselves are modified leaves: the petiole becomes a narrow stalk extending beyond the lamina, and at the end of this develops the pot and lid. The length of midrib between the regular part of the leaf and the pot is often long, and becomes tendril-like to grasp surrounding structures for support. During development while the lid is still closed, a slimy digestive juice is secreted into the cavity of the young pitcher. When this matures and the lid opens, insects (and sometimes larger prey) are lured into the pot to feed on the walls of the interior. The overhanging lip of the pot prevents their escape, and the smooth sides and downward facing hairs force them to slide down onto the liquid at the base, where they drown. Here, the enzymes secreted into the liquid begin to digest the prey, and it becomes a broth from which the plant absorbs nutrients that help its further growth and development.

Although pitcher plants may grow in a variety of habitats,

mentalized internally into a series of galleries and chambers inhabited by colonies of ants. Inside, the ants rear their broods. There are also other specialized chambers that absorb nutrients from the decaying corpses of prey caught by the ants. This is a classic case of mutualism, as both species benefit from their association, the plant providing shelter and sanctuary for the ants, and in return the ants protecting the plant from attack by various leaf-eating animals such as caterpillars, as well as supplementing their supply of nutrients.

OPPOSITE: *Common in heath forest, The pitcher plant* Nepenthes gracilis *may be the most widespread species in the Sunda Region.*

ABOVE: *The squat 'ground hugging' pitchers of* Nepenthes ampullaria *are distinctive. This species thrives in heath forest.*

RIGHT: Nepenthes rajah *grows only on Mount Kinabalu and Mount Tambuyukon in Sabah.*

like most other carnivorous plants the soils they grow in are deficient in nutrients, particularly nitrogen and phosphorus: their predatory tendencies obviously having evolved to supplement this nutrient shortfall. In most instances, in lowland areas, soils are sandy and acidic, often with layers of peat. In upland areas, soils also tend to be acidic and often shallow, but vary depending on altitude and aspect.

The range of sizes, shapes, colouration and patterns demonstrated by *Nepenthes* is remarkable. While the smallest traps on mature plants may be less than 2ml in volume, at the

opposite end of the spectrum they include the largest of all carnivorous plants, *N. rajah* that may exceed 2500ml (87.5 fl. oz.). Their most frequent victims are ants, but many other species of insects are also trapped, and the larger species of *Nepenthes* occasionally catch vertebrates like lizards and even rodents! Most pitchers are basically pale green to lime green in colour, but are often flushed with rich reds and purples too, some with purple streaks and blotches as well. The lip of the pitcher is often ornate, and has ribs and collars designed to attract insects and then prevent their escape; *N. villosa* and *N. burbidgeae* are particularly striking examples.

On Borneo, *Nepenthes* divide neatly into two groups according to the altitude they grow at. Lowland species grow from sea-level to around 1000m (3,280 feet), while those that grow above 1000m (3,280 feet) are referred to as highland species. Many of the lower altitude species are found in low lying heath forests, where soils are particularly nutrient deficient: more common species include *Nepenthes gracilis*, *Nepenthes mirabilis* and *Nepenthes ampullaria*.

The higher altitude group is by far the more speciose. Many of these species have very specific requirements, are found only within narrow bands of altitude, and have extremely limited distributions, as they have become isolated in certain montane areas. Lowland species, on the other hand, tend to have wider distributions.

Nepenthes taxonomy and classification is complex, not least because there are thought to be several instances where species hybridize naturally. Currently, 31 full species are known from Borneo. Mount Kinabalu is one of the richest single sites on the island, with 10 or so species, including unusual forms such a *Nepenthes lowii* and, perhaps the most beautiful of all species, *Nepenthes edwardsiana*. Mount Kinabalu is also one of the few places that a number of species are accessible and can be easily seen. On a walk up the summit trail to around 3300m (10,826 feet), one may find examples of *N. tentaculata*, *N. villosa* and *N. kinabaluensis*.

TOP: Nepenthes tentaculata *occurs on almost every mountain above 1000m (3,280 feet) in Borneo.*

BOTTOM: Nepenthes kinabaluenis *is a so-called natural hybrid species (between* N. rajah *and* N. villosa*).*

OPPOSITE: Nepenthes burbidgeae *is patchily distributed around the Mount Kinabalu area, generally occuring between 1200m (3,940 feet) and 1800m (5,900 feet).*

FOLLOWING PAGE: *The pitcher rim or peristome of* Nepenthes villosa *is elaborately adorned with highly developed 'teeth' that help direct prey into the murky liquid below.*

MONTANE FOREST

Montane forest begins at about 900m (3,000feet), when stunted oaks, myrtle and laurel become the predominant species. Ferns and rhododendrons are common, and with increasing altitude, heathers prevail. But on Borneo, and in particular, Mount Kinabalu, this environment is most famous for its enormous diversity of orchids, and at lower elevations, for the spectacular Rafflesia flowers.

As altitude increases, climatic conditions change dramatically, and this has a profound effect on the plant communities able to survive. Higher altitudes correspond to lower average temperatures; this in turn leads to the formation of swirling mists, as water vapour condenses to form clouds that regularly envelop the forest. Soil composition and characteristics also alter and change with slope and aspect.

However, because all of these factors are variable and interlinked, there are no hard and fast rules as to where lowland forests change into montane forests. For instance, on some isolated mountains that are laid bare to the rigours of the elements, the transition may occur at elevations as low as 600m (2,000 feet). By contrast, on more sheltered slopes on big mountains such as Kinabalu, forest with lowland characteristics persists to altitudes above 1200m (4,000 feet). However, on average, forests begin to show signs of transition to montane communities above 900m (3,000 feet).

Where this transition begins, members of the dipterocarp

ABOVE: *Fern species are abundant in montane forest areas.*

BELOW: *At higher elevations, montane forest becomes stunted and the canopy height reduces dramatically and becomes more uniform; species like oak, myrtle and laurel dominate here.*

ABOVE: *The Short-tailed Green Magpie* (Cissa chinensis) *is readily seen around the headquarters of Kinabalu Park.*

ABOVE RIGHT: *The Bornean Mountain Ground Squirrel* (Dremomys everetti) *is commonly seen above 1,000m (3,280 feet).*

and legume families disappear and are replaced by oaks (family Fagaceae), myrtle (family Myrtaceae) and laurel (family Lauraceae). These trees are typically stunted and more 'shrubby', and the canopy height drops dramatically to 20m (65 feet), often to much less. The constant clouds drench the forests in fine mists that encourage luxuriant moss and lichen growth that festoons branches and boulders alike. Ferns, tree-ferns, orchids and other epiphytes are common, and at certain elevations montane species of pitcher plant flourish. With increasing altitude, these characteristics become ever more pronounced, and members of the heather family (Ericaceae) begin to dominate; these include species of rhododendron.

In localities around Mount Kinabalu and the adjacent Crocker Range, the zone of transition between lowland forest and lower montane forest (800m and 1300m) is the haunt of a beautiful species of Rafflesia. First 'discovered' in the late 1960s, *Rafflesia pricei* was not actually described as a new species until 1984. Although not the largest, this is one of the most striking members of this very special family of flowers.

Animal life is less obvious and more specialized in these montane forests. Primates, for instance, rarely stray above 1400m (4,600 feet), as suitable fruit and foliage is scarce, although there is an exceptional record of a Red Leaf Monkey (*Presbytis rubicunda*) at 3050m (10,000 feet) on Mount Kinabalu. Yet some species of squirrel and tree shrew reach greater abundance in montane forests. There are also fewer birds, many of which are higher altitude specialists. Common examples include the Mountain Blackeye (*Chlorocharis emiliae*) and Mountain Wren-Warbler (*Napothera crassa*).

The Remarkable Rafflesia

Arguably the largest of all blooms, the totally parasitic *Rafflesia* flower is one of the wonders of the botanical world. It is gigantic, awe-inspiring, peculiar, rare and mysterious, and as such it epitomizes the exceptional and enigmatic nature of tropical rainforests. It is an icon of the plant kingdom.

During an expedition to south-western Sumatra in 1818, Dr Joseph Arnold and Sir Thomas Stamford Raffles were taken by an unnamed local guide into the forests near Bengkulu. The guide is reported to have said, '…come with me sir, come! a flower, very large, beautiful, wonderful!' In all probability Arnold and Raffles were the first Westerners to see such a bloom. When finally described in 1821, it was named *Rafflesia arnoldi* to commemorate both naturalists. The flower was so huge that, according to Arnold and Raffles, it measured a full yard across, weighed 6.8 kg (15 pounds) and held an estimated one-and-a-half gallons of water. Individuals found more recently have measured up to 95cm (3 feet) across, confirming that *Rafflesia arnoldi* is the largest flower known to the botanical world.

Other than their rarity, size and spectacular appearance, it is the bizarre lifestyle of *Rafflesias* that make them so fascinating. All species are specific parasites of lianas belonging to the genus *Tetrastigma*. The only visible part of the plant is a single flower that has no leaves, stems or roots. Within the host liana, all that exists of the *Rafflesia* is a fine network of filaments that penetrate right through the vine, but apparently cause it no lasting harm. Flowers of the genus *Rafflesia* are either male or female.

OPPOSITE TOP: *The cabbage-like bud of* Rafflesia pricei *lies apparently 'dormant' for up to 15 months before blooming.*

OPPOSITE BOTTOM: *After just 9 to 10 days, the bloom of* Rafflesia keithii *begins to show significant signs of deterioration.*

Flowers are assumed to be pollinated by bluebottles and carrion flies of the genera *Lucilia* and *Chrysomya*, which are attracted by the sight of the bloom and its smell, which

OPPOSITE: Rafflesias *bloom infrequently and unpredictably. Two flowers blooming next to one another is a rare occurrence. These two flowers* (Rafflesia pricei) *are both around 3 to 4 days old and are growing in the forests of Tambunan Rafflesia Reserve in the Crocker Range in Sabah.*

ABOVE: Rafflesias *are parasites of lianas, which are generally buried beneath leaf litter, so most* Rafflesia *blooms emerge on the forest floor. Occasionally, they erupt from the vine above ground level, as seen here, with a* Rafflesia keithii *growing on the side of a river bank.*

resembles rotting flesh. Much has been made of the smell produced by *Rafflesia* flowers: an early traveller once described it as 'a penetrating odour more repulsive than any buffalo carcass in an advanced stage of decomposition'; however, others have reported that any smell produced is exceedingly faint or non-existent. There are certainly differences in odour intensity between species, and also differences depending on time of day and temperature. In *Rafflesia keithii*, the largest and most pungent of the three species found in Sabah (see pages 16-17), odour is often at its most intense around noon, particularly on hot days.

What is certain is that pollination has to take place very quickly, as the blooms do not last very long. *Rafflesia pricei*, for instance, begins to show noticeable signs of deterioration after just two or three days, is in a moderate state of decay by eight

RAFFLESIAS: THE BASIC FACTS

Today the family Rafflesiaceae contains around 55 species, arranged across eight genera. All members of this family are rootless and parasitic, lack chlorophyll and are either monoecious (with both sexes in the same individual) or dioecious (with unisexual individuals).

There are 18 species within the genus *Rafflesia* that are distributed across parts of Peninsula South-East Asia and the islands of Sumatra, Java, Borneo and four islands within the Philippine Archipelago; nine species* occur on Borneo.

THE RAFFLESIAS OF BORNEO:

Rafflesia arnoldi var. *arnoldi*	Western Kalimantan and Western Sarawak
*Rafflesia borneensis**	East Kalimantan
*Rafflesia ciliata**	East Kalimantan
Rafflesia hasseltii	Sarawak (Samunsam)
Rafflesia keithii	Sabah and possibly Sarawak
Rafflesia pricei	Sabah, Sarawak and Brunei
Rafflesia tengku-adlinii	Sabah
Rafflesia tuan-mudae	Sarawak and West Kalimantan
*Rafflesia witkampii**	East Kalimantan

* includes species not seen for more than 60 years, that may now be extinct or that may simply represent variants of one of the other species.

or nine days, and completely degenerates to a mass of black slime by 15 days. Once inside the flowers, the flies are lured into hairy grooves on the side of the central column, which guide the insects against the anthers, where they are laden with pollen. The flies are then guided back to the outside world by the white spots or 'windows' that pattern the main bloom around its 'mouth'. For pollination to occur successfully, both male and female flowers must be in bloom simultaneously in the same area, so that flies can pass between them.

After pollination, the fruit is formed and seeds set. Dispersal of these seeds then follows (possibly by agents such as squirrels and tree shrews) and, assuming a host was successfully located, the seed germinates and infiltrates the vine. The first sign of the next generation of *Rafflesia* flowers is the emergence of a bud from the vine. This looks rather like a tightly packed red cabbage, and may emerge from a vine buried just beneath the soil surface, so the bud itself appears to erupt from the leaf litter. Alternatively, some buds emerge from vines above ground level.

The elapse of time from the buds' emergence to blooming varies between species, but it is always considerable. For instance *Rafflesia keithii* takes 12 to 16 months, while *Rafflesia pricei* varies between 10 and 15 months. One reason blooms

are so rare is that many buds die before they flourish. The causes of this mortality are uncertain, but may be linked with the host vine's inability to provide support and vital nutrients at crucial times, direct predation by animals like rodents and infection by parasitic wasp larvae.

Once a bud reaches maturation, it generally begins to open and unfurl at night, although the process may take between 12 and 48 hours to fully complete. From that point, the clock is ticking again if the next generation of *Rafflesias* is to be successfully conceived.

Places to See Rafflesias

Given their rarity and unpredictability, it is remarkable that anyone ever sees a *Rafflesia* flower in all its glory. But of course, they do. Two localities in Sabah offer a reasonable chance of success.

Numerous private plots are maintained by enterprising individuals around Poring Hot Springs on the lower slopes of Mount Kinabalu. These areas appear to be rich in suitable vines that are host to *Rafflesia keithii*. The owners of these plots nurture their vines carefully and protect any buds that develop. If one should bloom, a sign immediately appears on the main road that a *Rafflesia* is flowering, and they charge passersby a fee to see their prized flower. Make no mistake, on a local scale this is big business, as several hundred tourists have been known to see a single flower over the course of a five to six day blooming period.

The alternative site is the Tambunan Rafflesia Reserve in the Crocker Range to the south-east of Kota Kinabalu. These forests are higher in altitude than Poring, and support populations of *Rafflesia pricei*. There are numerous plots in the forest tended by parks staff, who monitor the appearance and development of buds continuously. Only if there is a flower in bloom do they allow visitors into the forest. The centre can be telephoned in advance to check the current situation. Both Poring Hot Springs and the Tambunan Rafflesia Reserve are a comfortable day trip from Kota Kinabalu.

Orchids and Mount Kinabalu

Orchids have for centuries captured the imagination like no other group of flowers: their exquisite form and vibrancy of colours have mesmerized botanists, both professional and amateur alike. As such, they generate a disproportionate level of interest and, because of the diversity it houses, Borneo is at the heart of this.

The orchid family (Orchidaceae) is probably the largest plant family in the world; current estimates suggest it contains a staggering 25,000 species! Borneo alone is reckoned to have between 2,500 and 3,000 species (i.e. 10-12 per cent of the world count) and at least 30 per cent of those on Borneo are endemic.

One of the major contributing factors to this immense diversity is the influence of Mount Kinabalu. As a family, orchids have adapted to a great many habitats, and are only absent from parts of the globe permanently covered in snow and ice. They do, however, reach their greatest abundance and diversity in the tropics. Mount Kinabalu is unusual in that in one locality, it provides such a range of habitats and climates, from steaming lowland rainforests at its base to windswept frozen peaks at the summit. Different

TOP: *Pendulous chains of flowers are characteristic of* Coelogyne rhabdobulbon, *a species common at mid altitudes on Mount Kinabalu.*

BOTTOM: Bulbophyllum lobbii *sometimes forms thick masses that ascend around smaller tree trunks. It is easy to see around the headquarters of Kinabalu Park.*

geological features further influence the soil characteristics, and features like stream valleys, swampy depressions and exposed ridges all produce different micro-climates at the same altitude. With variation in altitude comes variation in light, temperature and moisture that all further influence

OPPOSITE TOP: *The incomparable beauty of Rothschild's Slipper Orchid (*Paphiopedilum rothschildianum*) has captivated orchid enthusiasts the world over. The species is endemic to Mount Kinabalu.*

OPPOSITE BOTTOM: Phalaenopsis gigantea *is a large and spectacular species with sizable leaves.*

ABOVE LEFT: *The genus* Bulbophyllum *is remarkable for its diversity of habits and flower form. Around 90 species occur on Mount Kinabalu alone.*

ABOVE RIGHT: Dimorphorchis lowii *is endemic to Borneo: the flowers are dimorphic, with two different colour variations occurring along a single pendulous inflorescence.*

micro-climates. The consequence is a mountain divided into a myriad of climatic variations, and orchids have adapted to occupy each one of these subtly different niches. In certain instances, some orchid species become so finely tuned to the prevailing micro-climate that they only occur at one locality. There are thought to be over 1,000 orchid species on Mount Kinabalu; that is 3o per cent of all species found on Borneo, and a high proportion of these are endemic to the mountain.

Perhaps the most celebrated of these Mount Kinabalu endemics is Rothschild's Slipper Orchid (*Paphiopedilum rothschildianum*), considered by many enthusiasts to be the 'aristocrat of all the slipper orchids'. Such is its beauty and rarity that it has received tremendous attention from horticul-turalists and collectors ever since its discovery. Today, it is totally protected by law, and known localities on the mountain are kept as closely guarded secrets. Nonetheless, the astronomical prices plants command on the black market still means that there are attempts to illegally collect and smuggle the plant from the mountain. Five other species of similarly beautiful slipper orchids belonging to the genus *Paphiopedilum* are also found on Kinabalu.

THE WILDLIFE OF BORNEO

Borneo is part of the Greater Sundas region, one of the richest and most complex areas on earth. Over the millennia there have been dramatic changes in climate, with far-reaching effects on the fauna and flora: during successive Ice Ages, sea levels rose and fell several times. When levels were low, landmasses that are now islands were all interconnected: at various times, Borneo, Sumatra and Java were all joined by land to the Malay Peninsula. When sea levels rose, these land masses were cut off. More distant islands tended to be connected less frequently and for shorter periods. This resulted in fewer species colonizing them and, because of greater isolation, the subsequent evolution of a high proportion of endemic species. Other factors also influence wildlife diversity: climate and altitude are two. Borneo sits on the equator, and its climate is fairly constant, so seasonality has little bearing on the fauna and flora. However, changes in altitude can have dramatic effects. With an altitudinal range between sea level and over 4000m (13,000 feet), Borneo has a vast variance in climatic conditions, and this has contributed to a great biodiversity.

MARINE LIFE

The seas surrounding Borneo support some of the most lavish marine ecosystems in the world. Borneo lies within an area known as the Coral Triangle, that stretches from the Philippines through Indonesia to the Solomon Islands, and contains the world's richest and most diverse marine environments. Three quarters of the world's coral species and over 3,000 fish species can be found in the Coral Triangle.

The South China Sea, Java Sea, Sulawesi Sea and Sulu Sea buffet Borneo on the west, south, north and northeast sides respectively. The east coast drops to the depths (>2000m) of the Makassar Straits separating the island from the Indonesian island of Sulawesi. This channel constitutes one of the major sources of water exchange from the Pacific Ocean to the Indian Ocean. The Sunda Shelf dominates all the other coasts, with depths rarely exceeding 200m (656 feet).

The large rivers draining Borneo result in high levels of sedimentation and large estuaries, particularly along the southern margins. Sediment deposited by these large rivers limits coral reef development and produces large areas of muddy bottoms and broad alluvial plains. Mangroves, beaches and estuaries dominate Borneo's coastline, with only a few, scattered, small patches of well-developed coral reefs and islands. Coral reefs are most well developed around the northern Malaysian state of Sabah. Here, the smaller, shorter rivers carry a lower sediment load that results in the clear waters necessary for coral reef growth.

Coral reefs are concentrated along the northeast coast of Borneo, with the greatest concentrations in northern and eastern Sabah and in the Derawan archipelago of East Kalimantan. These areas harbor a high diversity of corals and reef fish, as well as some unusual features. In eastern Sabah, near the town of Semporna, Sipadan Island is Borneo's only island that is not part of the continental shelf. It is a small pinnacle whose sides drop precipitously to more than 600m (1, 968 feet). North of Sabah, the islands of Banggi, Balambangan and Mallawali are surrounded by Malaysia's

PREVIOUS PAGE: *The search for fruit is central to the daily routine of a Bornean Orang-utan (*Pongo pygmaeus*). This adult is feeding on ripe berries in Danum Valley, Sabah.*

BELOW: *Borneo's coral reefs are home to many invertebrates. Featherstars (*Chrinoid*), sponges (*Porifera*), and corals (*Cnidaria*) together create an environment for a diversity of fish and other life, helping to make these reefs the richest marine ecosystem on Earth.*

second biggest coral reef concentration. These islands and reefs link the reefs of Borneo to those of the Philippine island of Palawan. East Kalimantan's Derawan Archipelago is exceedingly rich; surveys have documented 460 species of coral and 870 species of fish along the 100km (62 mile) island chain. Kakaban Lake is the world's largest jellyfish lake, and home to four endemic, stingless jellyfish species.

All of these reef areas are threatened by overfishing, destructive fishing and coastal development. Throughout Borneo, blast and cyanide fishing are utilized to provide fish for the live reef fish trade and aquaculture. Reef surveys of Sabah conducted in the late 1990s documented widespread degradation of reefs with reduced coral cover, depleted predatory fish populations and a near absence of commercially valuable invertebrates, such as sea cucumbers and triton shells.

Management agencies and conservationists are working to reverse these degradation trends. Marine protected areas are utilized to reduce direct threats to reefs, restore depleted fisheries and allow for sustainable use of marine resources. Sabah has five marine protected areas, the largest of which is the Tun Sakaran Marine Park (350 square km/96 square miles). Sarawak has fewer strictly marine protected areas, but many coastal and mangrove parks complement Talang-Satang National Park, a marine park established to protect nesting sea turtles. In East Kalimantan, the coral reefs and islands are being gazetted as one of South-East Asia's largest marine parks.

RIGHT: *Coral reefs grow in nutrient poor, clear, sunlit waters. Gorgonian fan corals such as this are common on steep walls.*

BELOW: *Bannerfish are commonly seen on Borneo's coral reefs. They often travel in pairs as adults, and feed mostly on plankton.*

INVERTEBRATES

Tropical rainforests are the richest invertebrate habitats on earth, and those in Borneo harbour a dizzying diversity. It would be foolish to even hazard a guess as to how many invertebrate species are to be found on the island; in all likelihood it is countless millions.

Insects are by far the largest invertebrate class, and in recent years no fewer than 260 new species have been discovered in Borneo, with many more awaiting formal descriptions. Such discoveries have come from the detailed inventory of only a handful of sites; for instance, around one third of them have been found on Mount Kinabalu alone.

The Sangkulirang Peninsula in Eastern Kalimantan is an intricate system of limestone pinnacle 'karst', caves, cliffs and sinkholes. A brief expedition to the area in 2004 discovered a new species of giant cockroach that at around 10cm (4 inches) in length is thought to be the largest in the world. The expedition also found a bizarre semi-aquatic bug that lives in pools of water that collect in bamboo, along with several other insects and an unusual microscopic crab. It would be logical to assume that if other sites around the island were investigated, many more new discoveries would be made. In short, known species of invertebrate represent only the tip of a very large iceberg.

Insects

Insect life on the island of Borneo is bountiful to say the least; a single giant lowland forest dipterocarp tree may support over 1,000 insect species.

Butterflies and Moths

Borneo is famous for its butterflies and moths (order Lepidoptera), and is home to around 11,000 species. About 10 per cent of these are endemic to the island, and about 70 per cent are restricted to the former Sunda landmass (Malay Peninsula, Sumatra, Java, Borneo and Palawan). Many are surprisingly specific about their habitat preferences: in lowland areas, some are seen more often around coasts, others around forest edges and clearings, and some are only ever encountered within the rainforest itself. In montane areas, species also tend to choose either forest edges or the interior, while some seem to restrict themselves to the vicinity of streams. While there are no hard-and-fast rules, it seems likely that some of these preferences relate to the habitats of favoured food plants, not only for the adults, but equally importantly for the caterpillars.

OPPOSITE: *Few butterflies are more spectacular than a Rajah Brooke's Birdwing (*Trogonoptera brookiana*).*

ABOVE: *The Common Birdwing (*Troides helena*) is a frequently encountered species, often seen feeding on bushes in gardens.*

BELOW: *Exposed areas of mud by rivers and streams are often rich in minerals and sometimes attract large concentrations of butterflies.*

LEFT: *Borneo's forests are home to countless species of moth. The majority, like this unidentified species, are small. At night, a variety are often attracted to lights around rainforest lodges.*

BELOW: *The Atlas Moth (*Attacus atlas*) occurs in lowland forests and is a true lepidopteran leviathan. With a wingspan of 250mm (10 inches), it is larger than many birds. Males have huge, feathery antennae, the largest of any butterfly or moth.*

Perhaps the most celebrated group of butterflies on Borneo is the Birdwings (family Papilionidae): attaining wingspans up to 180mm (7 inches), these are the leviathans of the Lepidoptera world. They are also exquisitely beautiful, as epitomized by the famous Rajah Brooke's Birdwing (*Trogonoptera brookiana*). This is a species of lowland and low montane forests, and is generally associated with streams. Males are more spectacular than females, with scarlet heads and wings of jet black, with a series of iridescent yellow-green spear-shaped markings down their outer edges. It is not an uncommon species and may, for instance, be encountered in both Danum Valley and the lower slopes of Mount Kinabalu.

More widespread and readily seen are the Common Birdwing (*Troides helena*) and the Golden Birdwing (*Troides*

amphrysus) that inhabit both lowland and low montane areas. These butterflies are very similar in appearance, being strikingly marked with black forewings and bright yellow hind wings, although the Golden Birdwing is noticeably larger. Both species often visit blooms in the gardens of forest lodges and around forest edges. Also very similar is their close cousin, the Kinabalu Birdwing (*Troides andromache*); as its name suggests, this species is only found in higher altitude montane forests.

The family Papilionidae is a large one, and not only contains the birdwings, but also other familiar groups such as the swallowtails and mormons. Three species that are worth keeping an eye out for are the Common Rose (*Pachliopta aristolochiae*), Red Helen (*Papilio helenus*) and Common Mormon (*Papilio polytes*), as they often prefer forest edges, and can be conspicuous when there are suitable blooms. The Red-spotted Bluebottle (*Graphium doson*), on the other hand, favours stream-side habitats, and will often collect in large numbers on exposed river banks where there are minerals to feed on.

To add further to the list of heavyweights, Borneo is also home to the world's largest moth, the Atlas Moth (*Attacus atlas*) which can attain a wingspan of 250mm (10 inches). Its wings and body are characteristically a rich chestnut red, with intricate patterns and lines of black, white and gold. These include translucent triangular 'windows' on each wing, bordered in black.

The family Nymphalidae is another that is well represented in Borneo. Some of the most easily seen species around parks and gardens and on the edges of rural areas belong to this family: for instance, the Common Tiger (*Anosia genutia*). Also of this family is the Tree Nymph or Wood Nymph (*Idea stolli*) that is always found in forest areas and very much prefers the interior to the periphery. While the Tree Nymph lacks the gaudy colours of many of its relatives – it is translucent white with black spots – its huge size makes it every bit as spectacular. These extremely delicate-looking butterflies can reach wingspans in excess of 150mm (6 inches). Yet despite their fragile appearance, they are strong fliers, and can often be seen wafting through the canopy on slow, lazy wingbeats. They give the impression of pieces of tissue tumbling on a gentle breeze, and so are sometimes called Rice Paper Butterflies.

Stick and Leaf Insects

Another group of insects for which Borneo is renowned could hardly provide a greater contrast with butterflies: they are the insect world's masters of disguise, the stick and leaf insects, or phasmids (order Phasmida). Worldwide there are over 3000 known species; over 10 per cent of these are found on Borneo, and it is thought that the number of species awaiting discovery

ABOVE: *The slow wing beats and rhythmic rising and falling give the courtship flight of a pair of Tree Nymphs (*Idea stolli*), a rather balletic quality.*

may double this figure.

This group can be divided neatly into two: the stick insects that generally have long and sometimes very slender bodies; and leaf insects that are fatter and more flattened in appearance. Given the cryptic tendencies and very slim profiles of stick insects in particular, it might seem surprising that the majority can fly; only one third of all species are flightless. Their wings are neatly folded over their abdomens, and at times are brightly coloured, so giving a startling flash when initially they take to the air.

As a rule, male stick insects are shorter and more slender than females, and there may also be differences in body shape and colour. Indeed, in some of the flightless types, the sexes look so different that one would hardly regard them as the same species.

Phasmids are primarily nocturnal, and it is during the day that they use their exceptional ability to mimic leaves, twigs and bark to the full. They primarily avoid detection by not moving, holding their limbs parallel to the body and being virtually insensible to any stimulation (a state called 'catalepsy'). At other times they may also feign death (called

Baculolonga kirbyi, which can attain lengths of over 300mm (12 inches). It is also the world's longest insect: a specimen in the Natural History Museum, London, has a body length of 328mm (13 inches), and a total length, including its legs, of over 500mm (20 inches).

Being so well camouflaged obviously makes stick insects extremely difficult to find during the day; at night, however, they are active, and there is a much better chance of seeing them when they are feeding on their favoured leaves. Examples of the typical long, slender stick types are members of the genera Lonchodes and Lopaphus that are found both in lowland and montane forests. One of these species has a particularly evocative scientific name: it is called Lonchodes megabeast, and females reach up to 250mm (10 inches) in length.

In contrast, some species are altogether much shorter and stockier, and their bodies are often covered in all manner of projections and protrusions to help them blend into bark and twigs. Members of the genera Hoploclonia, Haaniella, Spinodares and Dares are typical, and many are endemic.

The leaf insects (family Phylliidae) differ quite dramatically from other phasmids, and are very distinctive in appearance as they all closely resemble leaves. Their bodies are green and flattened, with the extremities of the abdomen no thicker than a leaf. The legs are also flattened, and have large leaf-like lobes on each section to further enhance their clever camouflage. Only one genus, Phyllium, is represented on Borneo; females of the largest species, Phyllium giganteum, can reach a length of 150mm (6 inches), and have an abdomen 60mm (2 inches) in breadth.

In many instances, praying mantids are every bit as accomplished as phasmids when it comes to deception. But their deception has a devious twist, as it is not to avoid being eaten, but to avoid being detected by those they hope to eat themselves. The majority of these insect assassins do nothing more elaborate than imitate leaves; they are basically green in colour and slim in form, and often lie in ambush around the lights at forest lodges, where insects collect after dark.

Some mantids, however, have taken deceit to an extra level of subtlety. Thus, nestled amongst a beautiful and innocent-looking bloom lurks the Flower or Orchid Mantis (Hymenopus coronatus). Delicate protrusions on its body and limbs, combined with subtle coloration, enable it to melt into the form of the flower's petals – so any unsuspecting butterfly or other insect landing to feed on the flower is in for a nasty surprise. Equally impressive is the camouflage of the Dead-leaf Mantis (Deroplatys dessicata) that loiters amongst the leaf litter on the forest floor or rests on shrivelled leaves in shrubs. It, too, has intricate projections that appear like the crumpled edges of leaves in decay. The deception is near perfect.

'thanatosis'). Some species are even able to shed their legs (called 'autotomy') to avoid being trapped, although this also happens accidentally at times when they shed their skins. An example of the latter is Borneo's largest stick insect,

Cicadas

Anyone who has spent time in a rainforest in Borneo will be only too aware of the cacophony made by cicadas – a group of odd sap-sucking insects that are difficult to see, but can always be heard. Although there are different types that call during different times of the day, those species that begin their chorus at dusk seem by far the loudest. As soon as the sun dips below the canopy they begin, and it is almost so predicable that a watch could be set by it.

Only the males call, to try and attract the mute females. Their piercing, whining drone is produced by the rapid vibration of a membrane called the 'tymbal', which oscillates several hundred times a second. Behind the tymbal is a resonating chamber that greatly amplifies the sound. The call of many species is detectable up to 600m (2,000 feet) away, and estimates suggest that the noise produced by hundreds of

OPPOSITE TOP: *Slender stick insects belonging to the genus* Lonchodes *are numerous, but are devilishly difficult to find.*

OPPOSITE BOTTOM: *Male leaf insects (*Phyllium *sp.) have fully functional wings, whereas heavy females, like this one, cannot fly.*

TOP: *The Dead-leaf Mantis (*Deroplatys dessicata*) is another species that cunningly disguises itself like shrivelled foliage.*

BELOW: *Concealed within the petals of a flower, a Flower or Orchid Mantis (*Hymenopus coronatus*) waits patiently for a victim.*

cicadas in one tree is considerably louder than that produced by a pneumatic drill. Cicadas are the loudest insects in the world.

But this is only part of their lifecycle. Their eggs are laid into the stems or twigs of shrubs, and the hatching nymphs then descend and burrow into the soil to feed on the sap of roots. Some species spend several years in this state, gradually growing and developing in increments as they pass through several nymphal stages. As maturity approaches, the final nymph emerges from beneath the ground, pushing up a 'chimney' of soil through the leaf litter. It then settles on top of this newly created support, the skin on its back ruptures, and the adult insect bursts out, leaving behind a ghostly husk of its former self. Not all species emerge in this way; others crawl up trunks or on to foliage to cast their skins, and the empty cases can often be seen attached to bark and branches.

Beetles

When once asked what his studies of nature had revealed about God, the Edwardian evolutionary biologist, J.B.S. Haldane, replied, 'He showed an inordinate fondness for beetles.' Almost one third of all described animal species are beetles, and Haldane could easily have been referring to

experiences in a rainforest in Borneo. However, despite their abundance, they are not always easy to see. Many are nocturnal, while others hide away in leaf litter, rotting wood, or the recesses of the canopy.

Almost looking like the creation of a science fiction writer, the Trilobite Beetle (genus *Duliticola*) derives its name from the appearance of its larvae, which resemble the ancient trilobites that inhabited the seas of the world 300 million years ago. They live in leaf litter and feed on rotting wood. It is generally the females that are seen, and the biology of these bizarre creatures remains largely shrouded in mystery.

Amongst Borneo's most impressive species are the Rhinoceros Beetles (family Scarabaeidae, subfamily Dynastinae), found in both lowland and montane forests. Only the males develop the elaborate 'horns' that give rise to the group's name, and the males use these during bouts of jousting to gain access to a mate. Such encounters can be severe, and defeated individuals often retreat with large puncture wounds in their carapace. The most commonly encountered species is the Two-horned Rhinoceros Beetle (*Xylotrupes gideon*) that has a glossy chestnut back and black head. Much larger is the endemic Three-horned Rhinoceros Beetle (*Chalcosoma möllenkampi*) that reaches nearly 10cm (4 inches) in length.

Longhorn beetles (family Cerambycidae) are spectacular as adults, and gain their name from their extremely long antennae. However, they are renowned as timber pests, as their larval stages are particularly destructive. Eggs are laid on trees, and the young grubs hatch out and immediately burrow into the timber. They proceed to bore a continuous labyrinth as they feed on the wood and develop in stages. It may be several years before they mature and emerge as adult beetles, by which time they have caused serious damage to the tree, and in extreme cases, may have killed it. Although destructive to individual trees, it is thought this might help maintain diversity in the forest, as no one species of tree is ever likely to become dominant; were that to happen then it would be more likely to be infested and killed, and the balance would return.

Termites

More adept still at making a meal of wood are termites, sometimes rather erroneously referred to as 'white ants': while they are social insects like true ants (order Hymenoptera), they belong to an order called Isoptera. Termites are often seen as destroyers of the forest, when in fact quite the reverse is true: they are effectively creators for other species. It is true that they are the dominant arthropod decomposers in all tropical forests, but by playing such a pivotal role in recycling, they release nutrients for so many other species in the food web to then access. Further, termite activity such as mound building, excavating underground tunnels and soil feeding improves soil structure and quality for the benefit of others.

Termites live in colonies, numbering tens of thousands; they are based in nests, and the biggest termite nest ever found was built in Borneo by a species called *Macrotermes*. Different types of termite build their nests in different ways and places: some are underground, others are in mounds at ground level, some are attached to tree trunks and branches and some are even within the interior of the tree. The number of different species in Borneo is unknown, but probably runs to well over 150 species.

OPPOSITE LEFT: *A cicada emerges from its nymphal shuck.*

OPPOSITE RIGHT: *The male Three-horned Rhinoceros Beetle (Chalcosoma möllenkampi) is the insect equivalent of a Triceratops. Males use their formidable weaponry to joust with opponents when battling for a mate.*

TOP: *Bizarrely, female Trilobite Beetles (Duliticola paradoxa), so named because of their resemblance to fossil namesakes, retain their larval form even when sexually mature.*

BOTTOM: *The 'horns' of this longhorn beetle (unknown species) from the forests of Mount Kinabalu are verging on the impractical.*

Many species are adept at feeding on wood (something which makes them severe pests in timber plantations and wherever there is timber construction), and they have also evolved an ingenious way of utilizing lignin, the indigestible building block of wood. Inside their nests they cultivate tiny colonies of a fungus that appears like white pin-heads, and this fungus is able to digest the lignin. When the termites feed on wood, they extract what nutrients they can, and excrete the lignin. The fungus then thrives on the lignin-rich droppings, and later the termites feed on the fungus. The same fungus also produces enzymes capable of digesting cellulose, the major component of leaves. Once ingested, this enzyme acts on behalf of the termites, and they, too, are able to eat and digest cellulose.

Ants and Bees

Ants (family Formicidae) and bees (family Apidae) are true social insects (order Hymenoptera), and are also extremely numerous in rainforests. There are countless different species of ant, which may be predators or scavengers, vegetarian or carnivorous. Mount Kinabalu has possibly the greatest diversity of ants on earth: over 640 species have been identified from just a few hectares of forest!

Vast columns of these tiny creatures are commonly seen wandering across the forest floor, or ascending tree trunks. Some form nests under leaves or beneath bark, and if disturbed will swarm out to attack the intruders. Anyone who has inadvertently brushed against a colony of so-called 'fire ants' knows this to their cost – yet not all are aggressive. The Giant Forest Ant (*Camponotus gigas*) is one of the largest and most intimidating species in Borneo, reaching 25mm (1 inch) in length; yet it is harmless. The soldiers have huge pincer-like mouthparts to defend the nest colony, located underground, and they can often be seen wandering singly or in small groups with workers across the forest floor. At night, the ants climb from the nest to the forest canopy to forage mainly on honeydew, which is 90 per cent of their diet; the remaining 10 per cent consists of insects and bird droppings. Giant Forest Ants are very susceptible to environmental degradation and soon disappear from forests that suffer disturbance: as such they are an excellent indicator species for pristine areas and general forest health.

The Sun Bear (*Helarctos malayanus*) is one of the major predators of termites, bees and ants, and will readily raid nests, ripping them open with its powerful claws. These bears have an exceedingly long, adhesive tongue that can mop up the tiny insects in large volumes.

TOP: *The Chinese Lantern Bug (Fulgora sp.) is readily seen in many riverine and lowland forest areas.*

BOTTOM: *Giant Forest Ants (*Camponotus gigas*) are only found in pristine forests. Their disappearance from an area can be an early indication of deterioration in habitat quality.*

Other Invertebrates

Of course there are all sorts of invertebrates other than insects to be seen in Borneo's forests. While there are no deadly spiders or scorpions (class Arachnids) in Borneo (as far as is known), there are certainly some impressive ones.

Spiders

Spiders (order Araneae) have a wide variety of lifestyles, ranging from the classic web-weavers, to sit-and-wait ambushers, to active hunters. Many species prowl the leaf-litter at night, and wandering spiders (family Ctenidae) and huntsman spiders (family Sparassidae) can be seen easily, as their eyes reflect and shine like tiny orange lights in a torch beam. Crevices in trees are the favoured day-time hiding haunts of very large hairy spiders (collectively known as hairy

ABOVE: *The very large webs of Orb-web Spiders (Nephila sp.) are a feature of many forest areas, although the species is adaptable, and can also be seen in parks, gardens and around habitation.*

RIGHT: *Orb-web spiders, belonging to the genus Gasteracantha, have hard, flat bodies armed with three pairs of spines on the edge of the abdomen, some of which grow extravagantly. Because of their appearance, they are sometimes called 'thorn spiders'.*

ABOVE: *The maternal instinct in some spiders is strong; this female huntsman spider is carrying and guarding her egg case.*

ABOVE: *Large centipedes are formidable nocturnal predators, and eat a variety of smaller invertebrates.*

mygalomorph spiders, 'tarantulas' or 'bird-eating spiders': family Theraphosidae); at night they emerge to wait in ambush for large insects. Some individuals have a legspan approaching 130mm (5 inches); they are pale, fawny brown in colour, with silver guard hairs and a distinctive striped pattern on their abdomen. It is a consolation that these spiders are gentle giants, having temperaments not at all consistent with their intimidating appearance: they rarely bite unless they are severely provoked. Some indigenous people in Borneo call them 'gibbon spiders', as they believe they have the power to kill such primates (which they do not). Interestingly, and by comparison, spiders of similar size and appearance in West African rainforests are known locally as baboon spiders.

At the opposite end of the spectrum, Borneo is also home to the world's smallest spider: fully grown males of the species *Patu digua* have a body length that is less than 0.4mm (1/32 inch)!

The enormous golden webs of orb-web spiders (genus *Nephila*) may be 1.5m (4.75 feet) in diameter. They often catch the light streaming from the canopy in forest glades and along the edges of paths, and become a conspicuous feature. Sitting in the centre of the web is the impressive female, that may have a legspan up to 120mm (5 inches). She is both imposing and striking, her back often a mosaic of black with yellow and orange blotches, and her long legs translucent red. Examine the web closely and you may also see some tiny spiders in close attendance: these are not another species, parasitizing the lair of a giant, but the male *Nephila*; they can sometimes even be seen on the female's back. Some female spiders have a reputation for devouring their mates after copulation, but the male *Nephila*

makes sure that such a fate does not befall him by being so small that he is literally not worth making a meal of!

The large webs of Orb-web Spiders are constructed across open spaces, and are designed to catch large insects such as dragonflies, butterflies and even beetles. To snare and stop a large insect flying at speed, the silk has to be strong, and it is a true fact that the silk of *Nephila* spiders is the strongest there is, its tensile strength being twice that of steel.

Scorpions

Scorpions (order *Scorpiones*) are exclusively nocturnal, and are rarely seen as they spend the day in crevices under stones, under bark, in rotting wood or holes in trees. At night, however, they are active hunters of large insects. Very large black scorpions can sometimes be seen during night walks, often sitting partially visible on the edge of a crack in a tree trunk. These are collectively known as Asian forest scorpions (genus *Heterometrus*): there are over 20 species (although not all are found on Borneo), and some are amongst the world's largest, reaching body lengths of 80mm (3 inches) and total lengths (body plus tail) of 150mm (6 inches). Typically they have very large, heavy set pincers (called 'pedipalps') that give them the appearance of miniature lobsters. But despite their fearsome appearance, they are relatively harmless, and their sting is barely more potent than a bee sting.

Although they are also arachnids, whip-scorpions (order Uropygi) are not closely related to true scorpions. They are also nocturnal and feed on other arthropods, slugs and worms, and may be seen after dark resting on tree trunks. They do not posses a sting like true scorpions, but instead have a long whip-like tail that can spray a concoction of acids; this defensive mechanism is used primarily against small rodents and other potential predators.

Centipedes and Millipedes

Centipedes (class Chilopoda) and millipedes (class Diplopoda) are common in rainforests, and are often confused by the layperson. Firstly, neither group has as many legs as their name suggests: thus each body-segment of a centipede has one pair of legs, while each millipede body-segment has two pairs of legs. Most millipedes have between 100 and 300 pairs of legs.

Centipedes are nocturnal predators that feed on other invertebrates. They have powerful jaws and poison to subdue their prey, and some of the large species that may be encountered in Borneo at night can inflict painful bites and should be treated cautiously. Millipedes are often active during the day, and are vegetarian, feeding mainly on soft, decomposing plant tissue. They can typically be seen trundling through the leaf litter, or along a moss-covered branch. Some species in Borneo reach an impressive size: they may be 200mm (8 inches) in length, and can be spectacularly banded in alternate rings of black and red or black and yellow-orange.

Leeches

For many, the prospect of encountering leeches is one of the most unsavoury aspects of entering a rainforest. Yet while they can be an unpleasant annoyance, they do no lasting harm, and are not known to transmit any diseases. They are especially numerous in lowland forests, and can often be seen hanging from the edges of leaves by forest trails. As soon as they sense the presence of a passer-by – a potential meal – they begin waving to and fro, frantically trying to locate the prospective host. Most leeches find their host, gorge themselves, and drop off without ever being detected; the first inkling given is the tell-tale spreading blood-red stain on the victim's socks or shirt. The bite is not felt, as leeches are able to inject an anaesthetic, and the wound continues to bleed afterwards because their saliva also contains an anticoagulant. An exception is the Tiger Leech (*Haemadipsa picta*), instantly recognizable by its chestnut body colour with gold and black stripes. Tiger Leeches do not have an anaesthetic, so their bite is felt: it is a bit like a pin-prick. It does, however, have an anticoagulant, and a very potent one at that, as their bites bleed profusely, sometimes for several hours.

While Tiger Leeches and other similar species are relatively small, up to around 60mm (2 inches) in length, one species is enormous: the Kinabalu Giant Leech (*Mimobdella buettikoferi*) can reach a remarkable 300mm (12 inches) in length. Thankfully, however, there is nothing to fear, as it feeds exclusively on the blood of large earthworms.

TOP: *The Tiger Leech (*Haemadipsa picta*) is numerous in many lowland forests, and is often seen hanging from low vegetation.*

BOTTOM: *Giant millipedes are harmless inhabitants of the forest, and are generally seen moving slowly across the forest floor or along fallen tree trunks.*

AMPHIBIANS

The amphibians are unique amongst terrestrial vertebrates in that they depend on two separate environments at different stages of their life cycle. While as adults they live on land and breathe air, their breeding techniques are dependant upon an aqueous environment.

Not only do amphibians need to find water in which to breed, their immature larval stages – effectively developing embryos – need water to live in until they mature and metamorphose into adults. This partial dependence on water has restricted their colonization of certain habitats and environments, and has prompted the evolution of some remarkable lifestyles. However, where conditions are favourable, they have flourished and diversified spectacularly. Favourable conditions equal warm and wet, so tropical rainforests, like those in Borneo, are perfect.

Amphibians can be divided neatly into three major groups: the salamanders, the frogs and toads, and the caecilians, but only the latter two groups are found on Borneo.

Caecilians

Caecilians are a peculiar group that at first glance appear like giant earthworms; for instance, they do not have limbs, their bodies are long, thin, segmented cylinders, and their eyes are so small and hidden as to be virtually invisible. All these features indicate a burrowing lifestyle. Caecilians primarily inhabit leaf litter and soil, and the larvae of some species develop in the sandy beds of small forest streams. Not surprisingly, they are difficult to find and are rarely seen.

Frogs

In contrast, frogs are amongst the most familiar animals, wherever they occur in the world. Their consistency of body form makes them instantly recognizable: the more obvious features include a short, stocky body, long hind legs and comparatively short front legs, no tail (when adult), a wide mouth and big eyes. There are no vegetarian frogs; all species feed exclusively on animal matter, and for the majority this means insects and other invertebrates.

There is often much confusion as to the difference between

BELOW LEFT: *Endemic to Borneo, the Marbled Tree Toad (*Pedostibes rugosus*) is an inhabitant of hilly primary forest. This specimen was photographed in Danum Valley.*

BELOW: *The Poisonous Rock Frog (*Rana hosii*) is always found close to clear rocky streams and rivers. Its skin secretions can kill other small vertebrates, but it is not dangerous to humans.*

OPPOSITE: *The explosive metallic 'honk' of a Bornean Horned Frog (*Megophrys nasuta*) is a characteristic sound of lowland rainforest areas, particularly after rains. Few animals have evolved such a combination of modified body form and cryptic colouration to blend into their environment. This makes them difficult frogs to find.*

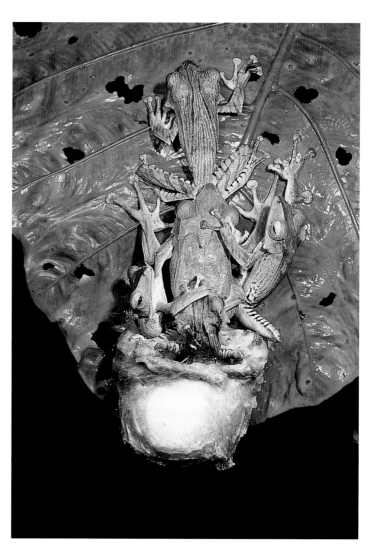

ABOVE: *Larger than males, female Bornean Horned Frogs* (Megophrys nasuta) *can be over 12cm (5 inches) high when sitting.*

ABOVE: *File-eared Tree Frogs* (Polypedates otilophus) *make a foam nest in which their eggs develop before hatching.*

frogs and toads. Put simply, all members of the order Anura are frogs, and the term 'toad' is generally applied to the members of one family, Bufonidae, which are characterized by dry, warty skin and short hind legs. Effectively, therefore, toads are a sub-group within the more broadly defined group, the frogs. Confusion arises at times when common names are assigned based on general looks and impression, rather than strict zoological criteria. For instance, the Bornean Horned Frog (*Megophrys nasuta*) is sometimes called the 'horned toad', as it is a large terrestrial species with short hind legs. However, there are also numerous true toads on Borneo (that is, members of the family Bufonidae) that all have distinctive rough, warty skin.

Like all amphibians, frogs – including toads – lay eggs without protective shells or waterproof membranes. Their spawn is very delicate and easily desiccates, so frogs have developed many strategies to overcome these difficulties. The

most obvious is that spawn is laid directly into water: this may be a permanent body, or small temporary pools, the edges of streams or even arboreal pools created in holes in trees. Some frog species effectively create their own artificial 'pool' in which their eggs develop; for instance, the female File-eared Tree Frog (*Polypedates otilophus*), a common resident of lowland forest areas, sits on large leaves or shrubs above water and creates a ball of foam by whipping up a mixture of water and mucus with her hind legs. During mating, the male grasps the female's back (called amplexus) and fertilizes the eggs as she lays them into the foam mass. This then hardens on the outside, but remains liquid inside, where the eggs hatch and tadpoles develop. Sometimes the whole nest later drops into the water below; at other times the tadpoles emerge and fall into the water directly.

One of the main features of night time in the forests of Borneo is the sound: it is never quiet. Frogs of many species are major contributors to this nocturnal chorus, particularly after rain, when breeding conditions are favourable. Frogs were in fact the first animals to evolve a true voice and produce noise by the movement of air across a series of vocal cords. After filling its lungs, the frog then forces the air into an inflatable vocal sac, which is either a single balloon-like structure beneath the throat, or a pair on either side of it. By moving air back and forth from lungs to vocal sac and over the vocal cords, a wide range of sounds is produced: trills, whistles, grunts, croaks, pops, warbles and chinks. Each species has its own distinctive sound and repertoire. Males are the principal songsters, calling either singly or in groups to try and attract the attention of a female. Some small species, for instance the endemic Tree Hole Frog (*Metaphrynella sundana*), sit inside hollow trees, the hole becoming a giant resonating chamber that dramatically amplifies the sound.

Where to Find Frogs

Frogs in Borneo fall into two broad groups: those that live in habitats created and modified by man, and those that can only survive in and around native forest. The first group contains only a few species that have learned to exploit rice paddies, cultivated areas around villages, drainage ditches and gardens. Not surprisingly, these adaptable frogs are widely distributed in other parts of South-East Asia, and none is endemic to the island. They include the Four-lined Tree Frog (*Polypedates leucomystax*), the Cricket Frog (*Rana nicobariensis*) and the Grass Frog (*Fejervarya limnocharis*), and species either accidentally or deliberately introduced to Borneo such as the Taiwanese Frog (*Hoplobatrachus rugulosus*) and Banded Bullfrog (*Kaloula pulchra*).

One of these ubiquitous species, the Mangrove Frog (*Fejervarya cancrivora*), is worthy of further mention as it is the only frog in Borneo known to tolerate a saline habitat. Because of their permeable skins, brackish and salt-water environments are normally uninhabitable to frogs. However, the Mangrove Frog is able to live in mangrove areas, coastal paddies and waterways that are obviously devoid of other amphibians.

The vast majority of Borneo's frogs are confined to native forests and adjacent areas. Most are quite specific in their choice of micro-habitat within the broader forest environment, because in this way they can tailor their lifestyle very specifically to prevailing conditions and reduce competition with species from neighbouring micro-habitats.

The banks of streams and rivers are prime frog habitat, and some species never leave these areas. The tadpoles develop in the running water, and later the froglets emerge and spend the remainder of their lives within a few metres of where they were born. Large, conspicuous species such as the Giant River Frog (*Limnonectes leporinus*) and Greater Swamp Frog

ABOVE: *The endemic Greater Swamp Frog* (Limnonectes ingeri) *is one of the largest species seen in swampy, muddy forest areas.*

(*Limnonectes ingeri*) live such a lifestyle. A variation on this is that some species, for instance the Poison Rock Frog (*Rana hosii*), live as adults along the edges of streams, but spend the juvenile or pre-reproductive portion of their life elsewhere.

A greater number of Borneo's frogs simply use a forest pool or stream for breeding, then emerge as froglets and hop off into the forest, where they spend the rest of their lives. The famous Bornean Horned Frog (*Megophrys nasuta*) is a classic example, and as an adult has evolved a sublime disguise to blend imperceptibly into the carpet of fallen leaves on the forest floor. Unlike many other frogs, this large species is not very agile, and is unable to leap long distances. With a stout, heavy body and short hind legs, it is only capable of very modest 'bunny hops', so instead relies totally on its camouflage to avoid being predated. Other frogs that adopt a similar lifestyle include groups simply known as the dwarf litter frogs (genus *Leptobrachella*) and large-eyed litter frogs

foam nests. Other arboreal frogs breed only in small bodies of water that collect in tree holes: the Tree Hole Frog (*Metaphrynella sundana*) prefers very small holes in narrow tree trunks, while the Cinnamon Tree Frog (*Nyctixalus pictus*) always chooses pools in larger tree trunks. There are even species that are able to dispense with standing water completely, and lay their eggs beneath leaf litter where humidity is high and constant.

One of the most intriguing examples of frog lifecycle and parental care in Borneo is that of the Rough Guardian Frog (*Limnonectes finchi*), a large species that lays its spawn directly into the leaf litter. This is guarded by the male until the eggs begin to hatch. The emerging tadpoles collect on the male's back, and he carries them around for up to several days until he finds an appropriate pool. He then takes his brood into the water, and they then swim off, to continue their development alone.

It is also worth mentioning that frogs are yet another group of animals in Borneo's forests that has evolved the ability to glide (*see* Flying Animals of the Forest, page 30). The genus *Rhacophorus* is a diverse group of tree frogs that are widely distributed in most lowland and lower montane forests. All members of the genus are excellent climbers, and have been observed and heard singing high in the canopy. At least three of these tree frogs are known to be gliders and are often referred to as 'flying frogs': Wallace's Flying Frog (*R. nigropalmatus*), Harlequin Tree Frog (*R. pardalis*) and Reinwardt's Flying Frog (*R. reinwardti*).

The pioneering Victorian naturalist Alfred Russell Wallace (see page 15) was perhaps the first to realize that a frog was capable of 'flight'. During a collecting trip in Sarawak in 1855, he was brought a Large Green, and the local who had collected it claimed it had flown from the trees. In utter disbelief and scepticism, Wallace took hold of the frog: "On examining it, I found toes very long and fully webbed to their very extremity, so that when expanded, they offered a surface much larger than that of the body. The forelegs were also bordered by a membrane, and the body was capable of great inflation...This is, I believe, the first instance known of a 'flying frog'."

(genus *Leptobrachium*), and also the White-lipped Frog (*Rana chalconota*) and the Harlequin Tree Frog (*Rhacophorus pardalis*).

Taking this trend one step further, the final group consists of species that rarely spend time near streams, and occur widely through a variety of micro-habitats in the forest. Most of these species live and hunt in leaf litter, and lay their eggs in temporary pools that form after heavy rain. Other species that spend the majority of their time in the canopy, for instance the so-called flying frogs (genus *Rhacophorus*), descend to the understorey to foliage above temporary water to hang their

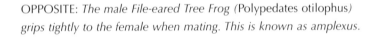

OPPOSITE: *The male File-eared Tree Frog* (Polypedates otilophus) *grips tightly to the female when mating. This is known as amplexus.*

TOP: *Male Tree Hole Frogs* (Metaphrynella sundana) *sit inside small water-filled holes in tree trunks to call and attract a mate.*

ABOVE LEFT: *Male Frilled Tree Frogs* (Rhacophorus appendiculatus) *form calling groups around marshes or pools on the forest floor.*

ABOVE RIGHT: *The Crested Toad* (Bufo divergens) *inhabits primary and old-growth secondary forests and lives amongst the leaf-litter.*

Indeed, all the three species mentioned have excessively webbed fingers and toes, which offer great resistance when open. Individuals are able to leap and spread all four limbs, splaying the webbing on their hands and feet to form little parachutes. By altering the position of their limbs, they can impart a surprising degree of manoeuvrability and control during their descent, even making banked 180-degree turns in mid-air at times. It is assumed that this is an anti-predator response, but it also allows individuals to descend quickly from the canopy to potential breeding sites, when temporary pools form on the forest floor after heavy rain.

REPTILES

It is not surprising that on a tropical island where the temperature averages around 30°C (86°F), reptiles are abundant. Being 'cold-blooded', they rely on their external environment to maintain their bodies at an appropriate temperature, rather than generating heat within themselves as 'warm-blooded' animals such as mammals and birds do.

The term 'cold-blooded' is an entirely misleading one, as the body temperature of active reptiles is often just as high as that of mammals or birds. More accurately, reptiles are described as 'poikilothermic' (or exothermic), which means they regulate their body temperature by behavioural means; that is, by basking in sunny spots when they need to warm up, or finding shady recesses when they need to cool off. Of course, the consequence is that reptiles are constrained by the climate and the environment: they are unable to live where average temperatures are too low, but where they are high, they thrive. Equatorial islands cloaked in forest, like Borneo, are perfect.

Just because they are abundant, however, does not

OPPOSITE: *Numerous islands off Borneo's coast provide secluded beaches where Pacific Green Turtles* (Chelonia midas) *nest.*

BELOW: *Large rivers like the Kinabatangan, Kapuas and Barito provide sanctuary for Estuarine Crocodiles* (Crocodylus porosus).

necessarily mean they are readily encountered or easy to see. Many species are secretive and/or nocturnal, and some are also remarkably well camouflaged. Even when they live in close proximity to human habitation, which a good number of species do, their presence more often than not remains undetected.

Nonetheless they are a diverse and fascinating group of animals, and on Borneo they range from the largest living reptile, the Estuarine Crocodile, to tiny geckos, skinks and blind snakes. Further, discoveries are still being made, and in recent years several new species of snake and lizard have been described.

Crocodiles

Only two crocodiles are found on the island: one is the False Gharial (*Tomistoma schlegelii*), a specialized fish-eater whose habitat is restricted to remote parts of Kalimantan and Sarawak. More widespread is the Estuarine Crocodile (*Crocodylus porosus*), found in coastal and brackish waters as well as large rivers throughout the island, although it is nowhere common due to centuries of hunting and persecution. Consequently, those animals that do survive are extremely shy.

Estuarine crocodiles are found throughout South-East Asia and Australasia, and have a fearsome reputation, largely because of their potential massive size, and also because there certainly *are* fatal attacks from time to time, although these are becoming less in Borneo.

Although this is the largest living reptile, monstrous individuals are now very rare indeed as they have been hunted so mercilessly. Nonetheless, the largest

specimen recorded in modern times may have been an individual known to reside in the Segama river in north-east Sabah in the early part of the twentieth century. The animal was well known, and considered sacred by the Suluk people of the region. On one occasion a British plantation owner, James Montgomery, saw the huge animal sprawled out on a sandbank near the mouth of the Segama. Once the leviathan had retreated into the water, Montgomery went to measure the impression it had left in the damp sand – and his measurements suggested the crocodile exceeded 10m (33 feet) in length!

It is possible to see Estuarine Crocodiles up to 4m (13 feet) along the shores of the Kinabatangan river. Even here, however, they are very shy, and it is unlikely you will be able to approach closer than 50m (165 feet) before they slip from the bank into the murky depths. Large individuals not only eat fish, but are also capable of taking mammals that come to the river to drink or swim across. Throughout Borneo, Proboscis Monkeys are often very cautious about entering water for fear of crocodile attack, and Bearded Pigs, which cross rivers regularly, can be easy pickings.

BELOW: *The spurs on the hind legs of the Asian Brown Tortoise (*Manouria emys*) are so developed that they resemble feet.*

Turtles and Tortoises

The waters off Borneo are renowned for their populations of marine turtles, and off-shore islands such as Sipadan (off the east coast of Sabah) are amongst the finest sites to see these amazing creatures underwater. Many of Borneo's off-shore islands are also extremely important breeding sites for sea turtles, and thousands of individuals return annually to the beaches of their birth to lay their own clutches of eggs. Four species are known to frequent the waters around Borneo, but as far as is known, two of these, the Leatherback Turtle (*Dermochelys coriacea*) and the Olive-Ridley Turtle (*Lepidochelys olivacea*), do not breed.

The most numerous species is the Green Turtle (*Chelonia mydas*), which can weigh up to 150kg (330 pounds). Less common and smaller is the Hawksbill Turtle (*Eretmochelys imbricata*), a species with a particularly distinctive and beautiful shell. Known breeding sites for both species are islands off the coast of south-west Sarawak, and in particular a number of islands in the Sulu Sea off the north-east coast of Sabah. Turtle eggs have been a prized food throughout South-East Asia for centuries, and continued collection on a huge scale, together with hunting for meat and their shells, has become a severe threat to long-term turtle survival. Realizing

this, the Government of Sabah officially protected a number of the most important islands in the late 1970s: thus the three main islands, Pulau Selingaan, Pulau Bakkungan Kecil and Pulau Gulisan, together with the surrounding seas and reefs, became the Turtle Islands National Park and the site of an intensive turtle hatchery and release operation. Further, in the mid-1990s the park was linked with nearby islands in the Philippines to become the Turtle Islands Heritage Protected Area – the world's first marine turtle conservation zone straddling national boundaries.

Both Pacific Green Turtles and Hawksbill Turtles breed within the park, although Green Turtles seem to prefer the beaches of Pulau Selingaan, while Hawksbills favour Pulau Gulisan. Turtles return throughout the year – indeed it is rare for a night to pass without some turtles returning – however, activity reaches a peak between July and October. On each of the islands, park staff collect all the clutches that are laid (each normally containing 60-120 eggs) every night, and transfer them to hatcheries, away from predators. Here the eggs develop in safety and hatch between 45 and 65 days later: interestingly, the sex of the resulting hatchlings is determined by the incubation temperature, slightly lower temperatures producing mainly males. The hatchlings are then returned to the sea under cover of darkness. On Pulau Selingaan, visitors can stay overnight to watch turtles laying their eggs, and to help park staff release babies.

Terrestrial species, which include soft-shell turtles, aquatic hard-shell turtles and land tortoises, are much less frequently encountered. There are around 11 species resident on Borneo. Species like the Asian Soft-shell Turtle (*Amyda cartilaginea*) can grow to a large size and weigh up to 35kg (77 pounds), but remain hidden as they live in mud at the bottom of ponds, slow rivers and ditches. The largest truly terrestrial species is the Asian Brown Tortoise (*Manouria emys*), that can weigh as much as 40kg (88 pounds). It is largely a lowland forest species, where it prefers areas adjacent to streams with a thick covering of leaf litter. Much of its time is spent buried beneath piles of rotting vegetation, and it lays its eggs in similar accumulations of leaves. Because of its large size, this species is prized for its meat which, as well as being highly nutritious, is thought to posses medicinal properties. The shells of this species can often be found in the villages of the indigenous peoples of Borneo.

Similar persecution faces several other turtle and tortoise species on the island. Wild turtle meat is highly prized as connoisseur fare, and is widely sold in many top restaurants, as well as openly in some markets. This especially applies to species such as the Malayan Box Turtle (*Cuora amboinensis*), the Asian Soft-shell Turtle and the Malayan Soft-shell Turtle (*Dogania subplana*).

Lizards

Lizards are the most active of reptiles and, therefore, more readily seen. This is certainly true in Borneo, where a number of species, both large and small, are reasonably conspicuous. There are also some very specialized and unusual lizards, none more so than the flying lizards. In all, the main island and its off-shore islets are home to around 109 species of lizard, the majority of which belong to one of four major families: the agamas (family Agamidae), the geckos (family Gekkonidae), the skinks (family Scincidae) and the monitors (family Varanidae).

The Agamas

Often seen around forest edges and in gardens is the Green Fence Lizard (*Bronchocoela cristatella*). This is one of the commonest species in the Agama family, and is a swift runner and excellent climber. If disturbed it can run quickly along branches and through foliage, before standing motionless amongst leaves where it becomes very difficult to see.

In forest areas, two similar agamas are also common and widespread. The Long-crested Forest Dragon (*Gonocephalus bornensis*) is an endemic arboreal lizard, the males of which develop an impressive crest running from the back of the neck down the dorsal ridge. Similar in appearance, but with an appreciably reduced dorsal crest, is the Short-crested Forest Dragon (*Gonocephalus liogaster*). Both species are diurnal and

variously patterned with blotches of brown and green, and some individuals may also be orange. They are primarily insect eaters. At night, they often sleep low in the understorey, towards the tips of branches, and are frequently seen during night walks in the forest.

The most celebrated of the agamas are the flying lizards or flying dragons (genus *Draco*), a group that is widespread in the forest areas of South-East Asia, but which reaches its maximum diversity on Borneo. These lizards have taken adaptation to an arboreal lifestyle to the extreme. Several pairs of ribs have become greatly elongated, and over these is stretched a membrane that is an extension of their skin. Most of the time these ribs remain collapsed against each flank, and the membrane neatly folded, but when the lizard needs to cross open areas between trees, it climbs to a higher branch and leaps, the ribs open to form a pair of broad wings, and the lizard is able to glide effortlessly across the gap, steering with its tail. Although this is not true flight, so accomplished are these remarkable lizards that they are able to glide distances in excess of 100m (328 feet). All species are cryptically marked and coloured, and so are very difficult to see when set against a tree trunk. Presumably this helps reduce predation, and if this fails, they can take to the air in order to escape.

Ten species of *Draco* occur on Borneo, the largest of which is the Giant Flying Lizard (*Draco maximus*) that reaches a total length of over 300mm (12inches), 55 per cent of which is tail. The majority of other flying lizards are much smaller; most are around 130-200mm (5-8 inches).

LEFT: *An adept climber, the Short-crested Forest Dragon* (Gonocephalus liogaster) *is often seen clinging to large tree trunks in forest areas.*

The Geckos

Gliding is very much a trait associated with the forests of Borneo (*see* The Flying Animals of the Forest, page 30), and the genus *Draco* are not the only lizards to evolve this ability. Geckos from the genus *Ptychozoon* have also developed a limited capacity for 'flight': in fairness it is stretching credibility to call them 'gliders' – a more realistic description would be 'parachuters'. Instead of 'wings', they have evolved extravagantly webbed feet and large flaps of skin that extend along their flanks and down each side of the tail; when opened out, these dramatically increase the geckos' surface area and air resistance, and so act like a parachute, allowing the lizard to cross modest open spaces between trees. There are three nocturnal species on Borneo, perhaps the most extreme being Kuhl's Gliding Gecko (*Ptychozoon kuhli*).

Geckos are also specialized in other ways, as many of them have the remarkable ability to climb even the smoothest

TOP: *Commonly seen around forest edges, the Green Fence Lizard (*Bronchocoela cristatella*) also ventures into parks and gardens.*

RIGHT: *The Leaf-nosed Agama (*Aphaniotis ornata*) is associated with primary forests, and is often found in the vicinity of streams. This specimen was seen on the banks of Sabah's Menanggol River.*

TOP: *The Giant bent-toed Gecko (*Cyrodactylus consobrinus) *lives in lowland forest, and is generally seen on tree trunks at night.*

BOTTOM: *The nocturnal Kinabalu Forest Gecko (*Cyrodactylus baluensis) *lives in montane forests.*

(10 inches) in length, and are common in forest areas and around forest lodges. They are sometimes difficult to see, but will certainly be heard, as their surprisingly loud staccato barks are distinctive.

One group of geckos on Borneo have lost their 'sticky' toe pads and instead have regular toes and claws. Not surprisingly, these are known as bent-toed geckos, from the genus *Cyrtodactylus*. All are forest species, and are beautifully marked with a pattern of dark blotches and stripes. On Mount Kinabalu there is a locally endemic species, the Kinabalu Forest Gecko (*Cyrtodactylus baluensis*), that is adapted to the cooler montane oak forests; it is regularly seen on night walks on trails around the park headquarters.

The Monitors

Monitors (genus *Varanus*) are not only the largest lizards in Borneo, but also in the world. The heavyweight champion is the Komodo Dragon (*Varanus komodoensis*), which is only found on the island of Komodo and its immediate neighbours in Indonesia. The largest species on Borneo is the Malay Water Monitor (*Varanus salvator*). This is a widespread, common and adaptable animal that is just as much at home scavenging around human habitation as it is in lowland forest and swamp forest areas. It is rarely found too far from water, and is an excellent swimmer. On land, large individuals, which can reach 2.5-3m (8-10 feet) in length (although 60 per cent is tail), may appear rather cumbersome and lumbering in their movements. However, they are capable of a surprising turn of speed, and can climb trees rapidly.

The two other monitors found on the island are much less common and more restricted in their distribution. The Rough-necked Tree Monitor (*Varanus rudicollis*) is confined to lowland forests in Sarawak and Kalimantan, while Dumeril's Monitor (*Varanus dumerilii*), which is strictly arboreal, seems to prefer coastal forests.

The Skinks

With nearly 40 per cent of the island's species, skinks are the most species-prolific family of lizards on Borneo, although the inventory is far from complete: in 2001 alone, three new species of skink from the genus *Sphenomorphus* were discovered in the mountain areas in north-west Sabah. There is little doubt that further species of skink await discovery.

Most skinks are small, inconspicuous lizards, some of which

vertical surfaces, thanks to highly modified toe pads that act like microscopic 'Velcro'. Anyone who has visited the tropics will be only too familiar with their presence on walls and around ceiling lights at night. These 'house' geckos, of which there are numerous species, belong to the genus *Hemidactylus*, and are now pan-tropical in their distribution. They are also highly vocal, and their clucks and chirrups are an endearing feature; in fact, in Borneo there are other, much larger geckos, that are particularly vocal. Species such as Smith's Forest Gecko (*Gekko smithii*) may reach over 250mm

are primarily tree-dwellers, while others are more regularly found on the forest floor or amongst fallen branches and vegetation. All skinks have a cylindrical, shiny body, with short limbs and a long tail. In some instances, particularly species with fossorial habits, this body plan has become extreme, and the limbs are dramatically reduced in size. It is easy to see how lizards such as these were the precursors in the lineage that eventually led to the evolution of the most specialized of all reptiles, the snakes.

On Borneo, the most extreme example of this trend is illustrated by the lizard, *Ophisaurus büttikoferi*, which is not actually a skink but belongs to the family Anguidae. It has lost its legs entirely and is sometimes referred to as the 'glass snake'; in common with some other lizards (but not snakes) its tail may break off and can regenerate (a process called 'autotomy').

Snakes

Few animals illicit such strong and conflicting emotions as do snakes: they promote fear and fascination in equal measure. They are embroidered in many cultures as symbols of malevolence, cunning and duplicity (in *A Midsummer Night's Dream*, Shakespeare spoke of 'snakes with double tongues'), yet in others as the embodiment of wisdom.

While these feelings are often irrational and the

TOP: *Rarely far from water, the Malay Water Monitor (*Varanus salvator*) often rests on branches overhanging rivers.*

BOTTOM: *This diurnal skink (*Sphenomorphus *sp.) was found foraging in a cave amongst the bat and swiftlet guano*

consequence of ignorance, fear is derived from the ability of some species to cause serious injury or even death through venomous bites. However, from a human perspective, the number of species capable of this is very small indeed, and it is sad that all snakes are condemned. Conversely, fascination is derived from their elaborate predation techniques, beautiful skin patterns and unique modes of locomotion. On whichever side of the fence you might sit, there is no denying that snakes are always compelling.

Many people in Borneo regard snakes in a negative way, and openly admit to their dislike of them. The Malay word for snake, 'ular', is readily used to describe someone who is unreliable, shifty or even sinister. And local Chinese communities call a devious person 'lau zhua', meaning 'old snake'.

Borneo has a rich and varied snake fauna, represented by ten families and over 150 species, with new discoveries still being made. Some are small and, because of their nature, very seldom seen – for instance the burrowing blind snakes (family Typhlopidae) – while others, like the pythons, can attain a huge size, sometimes live in urban areas, and are even prized as a delicacy. In rural communities, any python encountered invariably ends up in the pot, prepared as a soup or eaten as chunks of meat. It is even considered a remedy for asthma.

The Pythons

Borneo is home to just two species of python (family Pythonidae). The Reticulated Python (*Python reticulatus*) is another of Borneo's record breakers, as it is widely regarded as the world's longest snake. It is not restricted to the island, and is common through much of South-East Asia, Indonesia and the Philippines.

Stories of giant snakes are the subject of considerable exaggeration. During the golden age of exploration, Victorian adventurers and explorers were notoriously prone to report wildly improbable sizes for some of the snakes they encountered. In reality, accurately measuring a wild snake is virtually impossible, as they don't stay still and are too strong to uncoil into a straight line. Further, estimates based on skins are distorted, as the skins can stretch by as much as 30 per cent. That said, the Reticulated Python is known to regularly exceed 6.5m (21.5 feet) in length, and there are authentic reports of snakes reaching between 9 and 10m (30 and 33 feet), although such massive individuals have not been

LEFT: *The species name, 'reticulatus', given to the Reticulated Python (*Python reticulatus*), means 'net-like', and is derived from the snake's intricate geometric markings. Large pythons often spend long periods coiled motionless under hollow logs or concealed in dark recesses at the bases of trees, particularly after consuming a meal. This is potentially a time of vulnerability, and their pattern and colouration provides near-perfect camouflage in leaf litter on the forest floor.*

ABOVE LEFT: *The slender body and large eyes of this Spotted Cat Snake (*Boiga drapiezii*) betray its nocturnal and arboreal habits.*

ABOVE RIGHT: *Back-fanged and mildly venomous, the Mangrove or Yellow-ringed cat Snake (*Boiga dendrophphila*) feeds on frogs, lizards, other snakes, birds and occasionally, small mammals.*

reported on Borneo. On the island today, any individual reaching 5m (17 feet) or more must be regarded as exceptional.

Reticulated Pythons occur throughout the lowland forests of Borneo, and are often found close to water. When small (less than 2m/7 feet), they are primarily arboreal, and spend the day tightly coiled in secluded spots in the forest canopy or in tree holes. Larger animals tend to rest in hollow trees or under logs near the ground. They are nocturnal predators, and feed on a variety of mammals and birds. Large pythons are capable of taking monkeys, mouse deer and even Bearded Pigs. There have been records of fatal attacks on humans, but these are extremely rare. Nonetheless, large individuals are potentially dangerous and should be treated with great respect.

The Blood Python (*Python breitensteini*) is a much smaller species that rarely exceeds 2m (7 feet) in length, and is endemic to Borneo. It is unusually squat and heavy set for a short snake, and is renowned for being secretive and cantankerous. Despite being rotund, it is able to strike at prey extremely rapidly.

Typical Snakes

The majority of Borneo's snakes belong to the family Colubridae, often referred to as the 'typical snakes', the vast majority of which are harmless. A few do posses mild to moderate venom, and have long, grooved teeth (not strictly fangs) at the rear of the mouth.

Cat Snakes

One such group is the prominent cat snakes (genus *Boiga*), the most beautiful of which is the Mangrove Snake or Yellow-ringed Cat Snake (*Boiga dendrophilia*), glossy ink black with narrow, bright yellow bands. Its specific name refers to its arboreal habits, *dendron* meaning tree, while *philia* means affection. In fact, the snakes in this genus as a whole are typically long, thin and tree-loving, with characteristic narrow necks, triangular

heads and large eyes that betray their nocturnal habits. Yellow-ringed Cat Snakes are frequently found during the day coiled in trees close to and overhanging rivers.

Flying Snakes

On an island covered in forest, it is not surprising to find that a very high proportion of Borneo's snakes are primarily tree-dwellers. These include the vine snakes (genus *Ahaetulla*) and whip snakes (genus *Dryophiops*). Yet one group has taken their arboreal adaptations to an extreme not seen in any other snakes. The so-called flying snakes or tree snakes (genus *Chrysopelea*) are yet another example of a group evolving the ability to 'glide'. Two species are found on Borneo (with three others elsewhere in South-East Asia). The Paradise Flying Snake (*Chrysopelea paradisi*) and Twin-barred Flying Snake (*Chrysopelea pelias*) each grow to around a metre in length, have blunt rounded snouts, large eyes and are generally very brightly coloured. Not surprisingly, they are accomplished climbers, but can also launch themselves out of the tree-tops from a coiled position, straightening like a released spring and travelling through the canopy in a controlled, gliding descent. During the 'glide', the body is extremely flattened and the underside is concave, a position made possible by unique hinges on either side of modified ventral scales. The snake also continues to move its body in a typical serpentine manner, which helps prolong the glide and also allows for moderate control of direction.

Rat Snakes and Racers

Other prominent colubrids include the keelbacks (genera *Rhabdophis* and *Xenochrophis*), always found around water, and the rat snakes and racers, all medium to large snakes that are renowned for their speed. Rodents comprise a high proportion of their diet, hence their common name. Most are characterized by subdued colours, but two species are vivid: the large Grey-tailed Racers (*Gonyosoma*

TOP: *The Paradise Tree Snake (*Chrysopelea paradisi*) glides by launching itself from branches; it contracts muscles so that its underside offers maximum air resistance.*

BOTTOM: *An inhabitant of primary lowland forest, the Twin-barred Tree Snake (*Chrysopelea pelias*) feeds mainly on lizards and frogs.*

oxycephalum) are lemon yellow underneath and green above, while the Royal Tree Snake (Gonyophis margaritatus) is a checker-board pattern of yellows, orange, turquoise, blue and black, and is often said to be Borneo's most beautiful snake.

Venomous Snakes

Two families of venomous snake are found on Borneo: the cobra and the krait (family Elapidae), a group that also includes coral snakes, sea snakes and the pit vipers (family Crotalidae). While members of both families are potentially dangerous, the incident of snake bite in Borneo is uncommon (or infrequently reported), and fatalities are extremely rare.

The Cobras and Kraits

The King Cobra (Ophiophagus hannah) has a fearsome reputation throughout its range (which also includes much of South-East Asia and Indonesia), but in point of fact this is undeserved. They are certainly imposing snakes, often reaching lengths in excess of 4m (13 feet), and very occasionally 6m (20 feet); they are the world's longest venomous snake. However, these intelligent snakes are

ABOVE: *Although a common snake in most lowland forests, and even around the edges of gardens, the Grey-tailed Racer (Gonyosoma oxycephalum) is not an easy species to see, as it is arboreal and blends well into foliage. However, its bright yellow and green colouration and distinctive pointed head make it one of the most easily recognizable species on Borneo.*

generally shy, and being forest dwellers they cross paths with humans infrequently. In contrast, the Sumatran Cobra (Naja sumatrana) thrives around urban areas and on the edge of forest. It readily enters human habitation in search of rodents, and is frequently encountered. Although it is not aggressive, it should be treated as very dangerous. Bites occur mainly because they are mistaken for harmless species such as racers or rat snakes.

Other elapids on Borneo include a number of secretive, nocturnal species such as the Banded Krait (Bungarus fasciatus), which is terrestrial and is mainly found around coastal regions; and the Yellow-headed Krait (Bungarus flaviceps), of which there is a subspecies B. f. baluensis, endemic to the montane regions of northern Borneo, including Mount Kinabalu and Trus Madi.

Sea Snakes

Sea snakes (subfamily Hydrophiinae) are common in the warm waters around Borneo, and show a number of adaptations to their fully aquatic way of life. These include a flattened, oar-shaped tail, and the ventral scales, crucial for serpentine movement on land, are much reduced in width. They can also vertically compress their bodies when swimming. Feeding mainly on fish, they are extremely docile, yet they possess the most potent snake venoms known. Coastal fisherman regularly catch them in their nets and prawn trawls, but are normally quite happy to toss them back into the sea. Some species, for instance the Yellow-lipped Sea Krait (*Laticauda colubrina*), regularly come ashore on to rocky islets. One such place is an islet off Pulau Tiga in Sabah; these snakes can be seen here most months of the year.

Pit Vipers

Pit vipers have the most sophisticated prey detection and venom delivery mechanisms of any snake. Victims are located by a combination of taste and smell via the flickering tongue and elaborate heat-sensitive pits located in front of the eyes, which are able to sense the body warmth of victims. Their fangs are long, and hinge forwards during the strike to deliver venom deep into a wound. Unlike their cousins the rattlesnakes in the New World, Asian pit vipers have prehensile tails, characteristic arrow-shaped heads, and are largely arboreal, adopting a 'conceal and sit-and-wait' ploy

BELOW: *Wagler's Pit Viper (*Tropidolaemus wagleri*) is a nocturnal hunter. During the day it relies on its cryptic colouration, and lies motionless amongst foliage to avoid detection.*

when hunting. On Borneo, four species belong to the genus *Trimeresurus*: two endemic snakes, the Bornean Leaf-nosed Pit Viper (*Trimeresurus borneensis*) and the Kinabalu Pit Viper (*Trimeresurus malcolmi*), plus two more widespread forms, Popes Pit Viper (*Trimeresurus popeorum*) and the Sumatran Pit Viper (*Trimeresurus sumatranus*).

The most frequently seen species is Wagler's Pit Viper (*Tropidolaemus wagleri*). This snake is widespread on mainland South-East Asia, and is possibly the most numerous pit viper on Borneo. Because of its association with religious temples, particularly those at Sungei Kluang on the island of Penang off Peninsular Malaysia, this snake is sometimes called the Temple Pit Viper.

Wagler's Pit Viper is a beautiful snake, although juveniles and adults look quite different. Young snakes tend to be slender and vivid green, with a red line running through the red eye and bold white and turquoise bands down the length of the body. Adults are much thicker-bodied, and their colour darkens with age; they lose the red line on the head and the banding becomes more subdued. During daylight, they may sit amongst foliage entirely motionless, often remaining in the same place for several days. Even if they move away to hunt at night, they frequently return to favoured resting spots by dawn. Their are placid in temperament and rarely strike, but their venom is potent, so these snakes should never be underestimated and should be treated with caution.

BELOW: *Wagler's Pit Vipers (*Tropidolaemus wagleri) *are renowned for their placid disposition; however, they are capable of inflicting a potent venomous bite.*

BIRDS

Borneo has a rich and varied bird fauna, with over 620 species recorded on the main island and its outlying off-shore islands and islets, including around 430 breeding species. While this high level of diversity is perhaps only to be expected on a large island covered in rainforest, and with significant variation in altitude and habitat, the number of endemic species – that is, ones that occur on Borneo and nowhere else – is relatively low.

Depending on the taxonomy followed, there are around 39 bird species endemic to Borneo (according to *The Birds of Borneo (4th edition)*, by Smythies and Davidson; other figures vary, from 28 to 45 endemic species). This represents only 9 per cent of breeding species; by comparison, Madagascar, a slightly smaller tropical island also renowned for its biodiversity, has only 209 breeding species, yet a remarkable 55 per cent of these are endemic.

Why are these differences so stark? In short, the answer is relative isolation – or in Borneo's case, the lack of it. In the recent past, Borneo and its near neighbours, Sumatra and Java, were all joined together and connected to the Asian mainland, which allowed the free movement and colonization of mainland fauna and flora. The last connection was as recently as 10,000 years ago, and only continuously high sea levels after the conclusion of the last Ice Age have maintained the islands that

ABOVE: *The sight of a Rhinoceros Hornbill (*Buceros rhinoceros*) in flight is unforgettable, and the rush of air over their wings is audible.*

OPPOSITE LEFT: *The Wreathed Hornbill (*Aceros undulatus*) is often seen in small flocks, either flying over the forest or gathering in fruiting trees.*

OPPOSITE RIGHT: *The Rhinoceros Hornbill (*Buceros rhinoceros*) is synonymous with the pristine forests of Borneo.*

we see today; in contrast, Madagascar has been isolated from any continental land mass for at least 160 million years. In short, Borneo gains species' diversity by its proximity to, and recent connection with, mainland Asia, but loses out in the numbers of endemic species it is home to for the very same reasons. In evolutionary terms, 10,000 years of isolation is a mere 'blink of an eye', and no time at all for the moulding of new species.

Of the birds endemic to Borneo, it is not surprising that a significant number are montane species that have effectively become isolated on the handful of upland areas on the island, particularly Mount Kinabalu and other high mountains such as Trus Madi. These include some species that are relatively easy to see, such as the Bornean Stubtail (*Urosphena whiteheadii*) and Mountain Wren-Warbler (*Napothera crassa*), and others that are quite the opposite. Avian treasures such as Whitehead's Broadbill (*Calyptomena whiteheadi*) and Whitehead's Spiderhunter (*Arachnothera juliae*) provide only fleeting glimpses for the lucky few.

The majority of Borneo's birds are forest-adapted species that

struggle to survive outside forests, or where these have been degraded (such species are termed 'forest obligates'). Forests by their very nature are difficult places to see birds. Species that inhabit the forest floor and the lower understorey are often shy and skulking, while those that prefer the upper levels and canopy might be more inclined to sit out in the open, but rarely venture low down to where they are likely to be seen. This makes for frustrating bird-watching, and it may take several fleeting views of a species before a full appreciation of its appearance is gained; forest-floor dwellers such as the wren-babblers and canopy specialists such as barbets typify this.

The Hornbills

Nonetheless, there are some species that are boldly marked and conspicuous, and one such group is synonymous with Borneo: the hornbills (family Bucerotidae). Although they are found throughout tropical Asia and Africa, no group of birds epitomizes Borneo's rainforests more. Their large size, extravagant bills and loud calls make them instantly recognizable. In the larger species, the tops of the bills are often adorned with a horny excrescence called a casque. This is usually hollow and filled with spongy cellular tissue, and may act as a resonating chamber to amplify their calls.

The largest, and arguably the most spectacular species on Borneo is the Rhinoceros Hornbill (*Buceros rhinoceros*). It is the emblem of Sarawak, and also of Central Kalimantan, although it is not endemic, also occurring in Peninsula Malaysia, Sumatra and Java. Their call is one of the characteristic sounds of the Bornean rainforest, and is generally performed as a duet, where the lower-pitched, resonant honk of the male is complemented by the higher-pitched note of the female. These calls build together in tandem and reach a crescendo as the pair takes flight, the rush of air over the birds' wings producing an audible and repeated 'woosh'. They are usually encountered singly or in pairs, but several may gather together when a large tree is in fruit.

Similarly spectacular and large is the Helmeted Hornbill (*Rhinoplax vigil*). The casque of this species, while not as voluminous as those of some other species, is unusual in that it is solid, and the source of so-called 'hornbill ivory'. For centuries this was exported to China, where exquisite carvings were produced, and as a commodity it was more valuable than elephant ivory and precious stones, such as jade. Further, Helmeted Hornbills were targeted by indigenous tribes, such as the Melanau, for their extremely long tail

LEFT: *The Wrinkled Hornbill (Aceros corrugatus) is a rather shy species that may be seen singly or in small groups.*

BOTTOM: *A beautifully marked secondary feather shed from the wing of a Male Great Argus Pheasant (Argusianus argus).*

feathers that became central features in ceremonial head dresses.

Two similar species are the Wrinkled Hornbill (*Aceros corrugatus*) and the Wreathed Hornbill (*Aceros undulatus*), both of which feed heavily on fruit, and often congregate in the tops of very tall trees. The Wreathed Hornbill in particular may be very gregarious, with large flocks gathering at favoured roosting sites or particularly rich feeding sites.

When laden with fruit, giant fig trees act like magnets to hornbills (and a variety of other animals) that fly in from considerable distances to congregate and feed avidly. The large bills of all species are surprisingly precise and delicate, and are able to

ABOVE: *The male Great Argus Pheasants* (Argusianus argus) *is one of Borneo's most spectacular forest floor birds; its wing plumage and tail are the focus of the elaborate courtship display it performs.*

pluck and toss individual fruits one at a time. However, hornbills may be highly selective; studies have shown that they exploit less than 30 per cent of potential fruiting tree species in a given area of forest. Yet in favoured trees such as figs, several species of hornbill may converge at the same time.

In Borneo there are eight indigenous hornbills – the four previously mentioned, together with the Oriental Pied Hornbill (*Anthracoceros albirostris*), Asian Black Hornbill (*Anthracoceros malayanus*), White-crowned Hornbill (*Berenicornis comatus*) and Bushy-crested Hornbill (*Anorrhinus galeritus*) – and in some localities, for instance the Lower Kinabatangan, all of them are able to co-exist. This is largely due to their 'partitioning' of resources, different hornbills preferring different-sized fruits, and some also preferring to feed at different layers within the canopy. Because of their fruit-eating habits and their tendency to fly over large tracts of forest, all hornbills are important agents of seed dispersal, and are key elements in maintaining the ecological balance of the forest. That said, hornbills are not exclusive fruit eaters, and all species also prey regularly on lizards, snakes, tree frogs, birds' eggs and large invertebrates.

Hornbills as a family are remarkable for their unique nesting antics. The clutch of normally white eggs is laid in a large hole in a hollow tree. Just prior to laying, the female, assisted by the male, begins to plaster up the entrance with a mixture of clay, her own droppings, twigs and saliva. The large bill is employed as a handy trowel-like plastering tool. With the female inside, the entrance is reduced to a narrow vertical slit no more than 2cm (¾ inch) wide and 8cm (3 inches) long, and she remains imprisoned until after the eggs have hatched and the young are getting ready to fledge. For the entire period, she is fed through the slit by the male, and while inside, she throws out her own droppings and those of her brood on a daily basis. It is assumed that this extravagant level of maternal care is one way to best protect the eggs and young from potential predators such as monkeys, monitor lizards and arboreal carnivores, such as civets.

The Pheasants

In contrast, some of the island's other large and impressive birds are forest floor dwellers. The Crested Fireback (*Lophura ignita*) is a type of pheasant that may be encountered either singly, usually as lone males, or in small flocks of several females and one male. The male is strikingly coloured, his main body being deep inky blue, with large tail plumes of white or yellow and a prominent bright orange patch on the top of his back (after which the species is named). In common with other pheasants, he also has bright patches of coloured skin (sky blue), called wattles, around his face, that play an important role in courtship.

However, the ultimate courtship display, on Borneo at least, must be that of the Great Argus Pheasant (*Argusianus argus*). This large bird, where males may be up to 2m (6.6 feet) long (70 per cent of this is tail), is a relatively common inhabitant of lowland and lower elevation montane rainforest – although it is shy, so it is more often heard than seen. Its distinctive, explosive cry – '*kow wow*' – is one of the defining sounds of Borneo's forests: indeed, the evocative nature of the call has even forced its way into the Malay language: '*bagai kuang memekek di-puchok gunung*' translates as 'like an Argus Pheasant calling away on a mountain top', and refers to the hopeless longing of a desperate lover!

During the breeding season, the male Argus Pheasant maintains a dancing ground in a small clearing. This he tends with great delicacy, removing all leaves, twigs and debris to create a clear, unimpeded stage on which he can perform to potential mates. If a female wanders on to the arena, his display of extravagance begins with him walking around her in ever-decreasing circles until he is very close. He then thrusts his wings wide open, and inverts and draws them into a circle that creates a curved funnel. At the same time, he remains

BELOW: *This parent Black-and-Yellow Broadbill (*Eurylaimus ochromalus*) is flanked by two recently fledged chicks. A clutch size of two appears to be the norm for this species.*

hidden behind the wings, but waggles his long tail to produce a rustling noise. The long secondary feathers on the males' wings are spectacularly marked with lines of 'eyes', or *ocelli*, that form a bank of feathered finery into which the female is looking. However, she is not easily pleased, and may visit the dancing grounds of several males before she consents to mate.

Smaller, but no less impressive, is the endemic Bulwer's Pheasant (Lophura bulweri), a shy and patchily distributed species that occurs only in undisturbed sub-montane forests. During its display, the cock bird struts around, but stands erect and still when a female approaches. His striking blue face wattles then become engorged with blood, and forms long ribbons that dangle on either side of the bird's beak.

The Frogmouths

In complete contrast are the Frogmouths (family Batrachostomidae), another family confined to South-East Asia; this group of birds is rarely seen, but warrants mention because of their terrific camouflage and unusual habits. Not surprisingly, their name comes from their extremely wide bills and huge gape; in appearance they resemble huge nightjars, and have similar mottled brown and grey plumage, which looks uncannily like tree bark. They spend the day sitting very upright on a low bough, often at its extremity, and blend imperceptibly into the form and pattern of the branch. Only after dark do they become active and hunt for insects.

Other Species

Despite the obvious difficulties of bird-watching in rainforests, a good number of species can be seen during a forest walk in Borneo. There are always those that are confiding, brash or brazen, and make themselves plain for all to see. Forest edges in particular offer especially good birding, as birds often stop and perch and look out into the open space for foraging opportunities. As a bird-watcher, it is easier to be outside looking in.

The areas around the park headquarters in Mount Kinabalu are a case in point. First thing in the morning, the small patches of forest between the various buildings are often alive with birds, many species gathering together to feed. Prime locations are around the outside lights, where insects have collected during the previous night. Here, mixed flocks include garrulous Chestnut-capped Laughing Thrushes (*Garrulax mitratus*), Spangled or Hair-crested Drongos (*Dicrurus hottentottus*) and Short-tailed Green Magpies (*Cissa thalassina*), together with Bornean Treepies (*Dendrocitta cinerascens*) and Mountain Barbets (*Megalaima monticola*).

TOP LEFT: *Unlike their conspicuous relative, the Black-headed Munia, the Dusky Munia* (Lonchura fuscans) *tends to be rather unobtrusive. They are common around forest edges and rice paddies.*

BOTTOM LEFT: *The Black-and-Red Broadbill* (Eurylaimus macrorhynchos) *constructs a large, untidy pear-shaped nest (typical of broadbills), often overhanging streams or small rivers.*

ABOVE RIGHT: *Widely but sparsely distributed throughout Borneo, Storm's Stork* (Ciconia stormi) *frequents forest areas close to rivers, and constructs large nests at the tops of tall trees.*

Wherever there are flowers blooming, smaller species such as sunbirds, flowerpeckers and Mountain Tailorbirds (*Orthotomus cuculatus*) often congregate, and Indigo Flycatchers (*Eumyias indigo*) sally out from branches to intercept unsuspecting insects on the wing, while on branches just beneath, a male White-throated Fantail (*Rhipidura albicollis*) might perform a flitting dance routine.

Similarly, the areas around Borneo Rainforest Lodge in

TOP: *The Blue-winged Pitta (*Pitta moluccensis*) is a passage migrant and non-breeding visitor to Borneo.*

LEFT: *One of five pitta species occurring in Danum Valley, the Banded Pitta (*Pitta guajana*) can be difficult to see.*

OPPOSITE: *The Stork-billed Kingfisher (*Halcyon capensis*) is the largest kingfisher in Borneo, and is a common resident along most major rivers and tidal creeks. A shy bird, it is hard to approach.*

Danum Valley offer a window into the world of some of the commoner bird species of lowland forests. Where there are flowers, the Grey-breasted Spiderhunter (*Arachnothera affinis*) can often be seen probing for a meal, and the strikingly marked Black-and-Red Broadbill (*Cymbirhynchus macrorhynchos*) and Black-and-Yellow Broadbill (*Eurylaimus ochromalus*) often sit motionless on a prominent perch. Further, mixed flocks of bulbuls provide an identity challenge to the keen bird watcher, as do the numerous species of babbler that are frequently encountered flitting around the understorey.

The Pittas

Perhaps the ultimate bird-watching challenge in Danum (or any other forest areas, for that matter) is to track down what is arguably Borneo's most sought-after group of birds, the pittas (family Pittidae). Such is the impact of their brilliant plumage and exquisite beauty that for many, pittas have become the bird-watching equivalent of precious gems. Add to this their shyness, their penchant for skulking in the darkest of rainforest recesses, and in some instances, their rarity, and their allure is compounded.

Although two species reside in Africa and one in Peninsula India, the pittas comprise a family that characteristically inhabits the various humid forest types of South-East Asia and Australasia. In all, nine species are found on Borneo, and three of these are endemic (though some authorities quote two endemic species, regarding the Black-headed Pitta – *Pitta ussheri* – as synonymous with the Garnet Pitta – *Pitta granatina*, see below). Finding pittas is often a tough proposition, as their piercing, high-pitched whistles and calls are very difficult to pin-point, but from time to time one may be found hopping down a forest trail early in the morning. Danum is one of the island's most species-rich sites, and is home to the endemic Black-headed Pitta (*Pitta ussheri*) and Blue-headed Pitta (*Pitta baudii*), plus three more widespread species, the Giant Pitta (*Pitta caerulea*), Banded Pitta (*Pitta guajana*) and Hooded Pitta (*Pitta sordida*).

The third endemic species is the Blue-banded Pitta (*Pitta arquata*), which seems to prefer higher altitude forests, especially where bamboo is common; it is known from scattered localities in Kalimantan, Sarawak and Sabah. In contrast, the Garnet Pitta (*Pitta granatina*) is widespread, and is also found on Sumatra, Peninsula Malaysia and Thailand. It is very similar in appearance and habits to the endemic Black-headed Pitta, but on Borneo their ranges do not overlap. Both remaining species, the Fairy Pitta (*Pitta nympha*) and Blue-winged Pitta (*Pitta moluccensis*), are migratory, only visiting Borneo outside their breeding season.

The Swiftlet and Birds' Nest Soup

There are probably few potentially edible things that humans have not tried to eat at one time or another, but the concept of soup made from the nest of a bird has to be one of the most bizarre. The Chinese penchant for birds' nest soup dates back over 1,000 years, and when the first Europeans reached South-East Asia and Borneo (c. 1600), the trade in nests was flourishing. Such was their value that during the 18th and 19th centuries, the increasing nest trade made significant contributions to the emerging economies of South-East Asia in general and Borneo in particular.

The demand today is greater than ever, with China and overseas Chinese communities prepared to pay high prices for

BELOW: *Three times a year, collectors climb to the roof of the Gomantong Caves in Sabah to harvest swiftlet nests.*

the raw material, to supply their restaurants. But what exactly is the raw material? And from where does it come?

The nests are those of tiny swiftlets belonging to the genus *Aerodramus*. Two species in particular are of commercial importance, the more valued White-nest Swiftlet (*A. fuciphagus*), which is less numerous in Borneo, and the more common Black-nest Swiftlet (*A. maximus*). These birds nest in colonies in large caves in truly enormous numbers: in the largest caves there may be several million birds — for instance, there are an estimated one million pairs in the Great Cave at Niah in Sarawak alone.

ABOVE: *Nests from the Black-nest Swiflet (*Aerodramus maximus) *are less highly prized than those of their white-nest counterparts, but they still provide a resource of significant economic importance.*

The risks that collectors are willing to take when harvesting the nests reflects the value placed upon them. Using traditionally crafted rattan and rope ladders and bamboo poles, collectors ascend to the cave roofs, often 60m (195 feet), where the swiftlets cement their tiny cup nests to the rock. The nests are scraped from the roof with a tool called a *jalok,* essentially an iron blade mounted on a long bamboo handle. The nests then fall to the floor, where they are collected by other members of the team.

Most swifts use glutinous secretions produced from the mouth to bind together materials for their nests. In some swiftlets, this salivary cement constitutes a significant proportion of the nest, and it is this that is highly prized as an ingredient. White nests (from *A. fuciphagus*) are the most valuable, as they are constructed almost exclusively of salivary material, with only a few feathers attached to the nest. Less valuable are black nests (from *A. maximus*), in which the salivary component is mixed with a variety of feathers from the swiftlet's plumage. Although caves often contain the nests of both species, it is normal for one or the other to predominate.

Between the cave roof and the soup bowl, the nests must be auctioned to traders, soaked and washed, the dirt removed, dried in the sun and compressed into small, thin pancakes for shipping. In this desiccated state they will keep for several years. Before serving, the nests are soaked again and boiled, then incorporated into soups, generally with either chicken, fish or shellfish. The Chinese have long believed that the nests have medicinal qualities (studies have shown that the saliva does contain some important amino acids), but whether this ingredient imparts any discernible flavour is debatable; some

have described the filaments as 'semi-transparent, colourless and tasteless'. Nevertheless its financial value is undeniable; the 'white' nests can fetch upwards of US$4,000 per kilo (in 2005), while 'black' nests are worth around half this after cleaning. Affluent diners at thousands of Chinese restaurants obviously think it is a delicacy worth paying for: a bowl of soup containing only fractional quantities of the nest ingredient can cost from US$25 upwards.

At the opposite end of the market chain, the nest collectors earn but a fraction of such sums. Nonetheless, to a collector a handful of nests – and particularly the more valuable white nests – might be worth many months regular salary. As such, the caves are jealously guarded by the collecting communities.

In all areas of Borneo where there are swiftlet populations, there are national, State and provincial regulations to protect the birds and control their exploitation. For instance, in Sabah, the collection of nests from the cave systems at Gomantong is strictly monitored to ensure sustainability, and many believe these to be the best managed birds'-nest caves in the world.

At the onset of the breeding season, the swiflets construct a nest, and this is harvested immediately. The birds then build a second nest and are left to their own devices until after the chicks have fledged. The vacated nests are then collected. The breeding season of the two main commercial swiftlet species varies, and there are differences between cave systems — even from cave to cave. At Simud Putih cave in Gomantong, the initial harvest of 'white' nests is in February, followed by the second collection in June or July; whereas in the main cave, Simud Hitam, first collections are in March and April, then again in late August and September.

Controls are seemingly ineffective, however, and swiftlet populations throughout Borneo are on the decline due to two factors. Firstly, rising demand and escalating prices for nests has led to increased pressure on collectors to provide the commodity, resulting in over-harvesting and mismanagement of some cave systems. And secondly, forest clearance and conversion to crops has detrimentally affected the insect populations on which the swiflets feed, causing decline independently of nest harvesting. To counter this, attempts are currently being made to cultivate nesting colonies in purpose-built structures.

Mammals

Twelve terrestrial mammalian orders are represented on Borneo (excluding cetaceans), and these range from familiar groups, such as primates and rodents, to oddities like the armoured Pangolin and the peculiar Colugo, or Flying Lemur.

In total, these diverse groups contain approximately 222 species. However, compared to many other animal groups, the island's mammals are understudied. Bats, for example, make up nearly half of most tropical forest mammal communities, and as pollinators and agents of seed dispersal, they play a crucial role in forest regeneration. However, few complete surveys have been undertaken on Borneo, and bat communities from the forest interior are unknown.

The case is similar for other small mammals that are known to occur in complex communities with high levels of species richness, yet little else is known. This paucity of knowledge is

no doubt linked to the difficulties of working for prolonged periods in the rainforest environment, and because so many small mammals are cryptic, nocturnal or secretive.

On an island dominated by forest it is not surprising that there is a heavy bias towards species adapted to a life in the trees or flying between them. Many species are arboreal and spend the majority of their time in the canopy; these include monkeys, apes, most squirrels, some carnivores and tree shrews. Other species are at least partially arboreal, splitting their time between the forest floor and the canopy; many of the carnivores conform here, for instance several of the civets and the cats. Other larger mammals tend to be completely terrestrial, including pigs, deer and the very largest species, rhinos and elephants. Further, over 40 per cent of the island's mammal species are bats, and some of the cave systems on the island (the largest in the world) are amongst the richest bat sites anywhere.

The greatest mammal diversity is found in lowland dipterocarp rainforest and riverine forest, with fewer species occurring in swamp forest or kerangas forest. Some more specialized species are restricted to higher elevations in montane forest. Perhaps surprisingly, a number of species appear to be adaptable enough to survive in altered habitats, and can be encountered in logged forest, secondary forest and sometimes even plantations. Forest edges, where primary habitat adjoins plantations or gardens, often support relatively high densities. A high proportion of Borneo's mammals are also nocturnal and spend the daylight hours tucked away in tree holes or caves, and consequently are difficult to observe. These include flying squirrels, bats, rodents, most of the small carnivores and two species of primate.

LEFT: *Large cave systems, like those at Gomantong in Sabah, provide refuge for numerous species of bats.*

OPPOSITE: *The Slow Loris (*Nycticebus coucang*) is a common but infrequently seen inhabitant of lowland and lower montane rainforest. It is exclusively nocturnal.*

Borneo's forests are criss-crossed with a latticework of rivers, large and small, and many of the larger ones appear to be important in determining the distribution of some mammals, because they act as natural barriers. Often, these rivers are effective boundaries separating one species or subspecies from another – for instance, the Kapuas and Barito rivers that separate the ranges of the Bornean and Agile Gibbon.

Bats

Bats are unique amongst mammals in that they are capable of true flight. While other species on Borneo are inaccurately described as 'flying', for instance, the flying squirrels and flying lemur (Colugo), they are in fact only able to glide, and have no means of generating power and propulsion. Over 90 species of bat occur on the island of Borneo.

Bats are also remarkable in that they form the largest aggregations of any mammal; in some parts of the world, single-species colonies of between 20 and 50 million have been recorded in caves (for example, the Brazilian Free-tailed Bats in Texas). While known colonies in Borneo do not approach these figures, the caves at Gunung Mulu, Niah and Gomantong, for instance, all support mixed-species colonies of several million bats, certainly the largest mammal congregations on Borneo. At dusk, when they emerge in great streams, it appears as though plumes of smoke are rising from the cave entrance.

Bats can be divided neatly into two main groups and both

ABOVE: *The Large Tree Shrew (*Tupaia tana*) is diurnal and mainly terrestrial. It feeds on arthropods, earthworms and some fruit.*

OPPOSITE: *The Lesser Gymnure (*Hylomys suillus*) is a small insectivore that lives in montane forests. It is largely diurnal and terrestrial.*

occur on Borneo. The largest species are the fruit bats (suborder Megachiroptera, family Pteropodidae) that feed mainly on fruits and nectar; they rely primarily on sight, and do not have the complex echolocation mechanisms of smaller bats (the genus *Rousettus* is an exception, as they possess rudimentary echolocation capabilities).

Some of the largest fruit bats have a long muzzle and very dog-like features, which gives rise to their alternative common name, the flying foxes. There are just two species resident on Borneo; the Large Flying Fox (*Pteropus vampyrus*), with a wingspan of over 1.2m (4 feet), is the island's largest bat, and is found mainly in lowland forest areas. Some colonies roost in coastal mangroves and nipah forest. The second, smaller species is the Island Flying Fox (*Pteropus hypomelanus*), and as its name suggests, it is found mainly on off-shore islands, where it roosts in the fronds of coconut palms and the branches of similar trees. This species can easily be seen on Selingan Island, within the Turtle Islands National Park, near Sandakan in Sabah.

Other fruit bats in Borneo, of which there are fifteen species, are generally forest dwellers, and roost in tall trees, and sometimes the entrances to caves. Some, like the Short-nosed

Fruit Bat (*Cynopterus brachyotis*) and Dusky Fruit Bat (*Penthetor lucasi*), are common and widespread throughout the island, whereas others, for instance the White-collared Fruit Bat (*Megaerops wetmorei*) and Black-capped Fruit Bat (*Chironax melanocephalus*), are known only from odd records at scattered localities.

The vast majority of bats on Borneo belong to the second major grouping, the micro bats (suborder Microchiroptera), all of which have evolved the capability to echolocate as a means of navigation and finding their prey. This means that all have relatively large ears, and many have developed very elaborate flaps and growths of skin around the face, referred to as 'nose-leafs'. In most species, prey primarily consists of insects caught on the wing. The smallest species, such as the Least Woolly Bat (*Kerivoula minuta*)

and the Small-toothed Mouse-eared Bat (*Myotis siligorensis*), weigh little more than 2g (0.07 ounces), while the larger species such as Tome's False Serotine (*Hesperoptenus tomesi*) can weigh over 20g (0.7 ounces). However, in all instances, identifying micro bats is very difficult (or impossible) without catching and examining individuals at close quarters.

Insectivores and Tree Shrews

Few animals have a more unearthly appearance than the Moonrat (*Echinosorex gymnurus*). It is a close relative of the hedgehog, but instead of being covered in spines, it is cloaked in a ghostly coat of pure white fur. Moonrats are insectivores (order Lipotyphla), and behave in many respects like their cousins, the shrews. Little is known of their habits, other than that they are nocturnal and terrestrial, and spend the day asleep in burrows. Their diet is dominated by earthworms and small arthropods. Although they are known to venture into gardens and plantations on the mainland, on Borneo they appear to prefer forest environments.

Several true shrews (family Soricidae) also occur on Borneo. Shrews include the smallest of mammals, other than bats, and also have the highest metabolic rates; in some instances their heart beats at over 1,000 times per minute (the resting average for a human is 70 to 80 beats per minute). This translates to a voracious appetite, and most species have to eat at least every couple of hours.

Tree shrews superficially resemble insectivores or small

squirrels, but in fact belong to their own separate group (order Scandentia) that is largely restricted to the forests of South-East Asia. Their common name is certainly misleading, as most species are not particularly adept climbers, and some are mainly terrestrial. Borneo is home to the greatest diversity of tree shrews, with 10 out of the 18 species occurring on the island. This probably indicates that Borneo was their centre of evolution, and provided the platform for their subsequent adaptive radiation. Certainly, Borneo's large size and diversity of habitats have contributed to the evolution of the numerous species on the island.

In lowland forest areas, the most regularly encountered species is the Common Tree Shrew (*Tupaia glis*); its coat is uniformly ruddy brown, and it has a characteristic pointed snout and bushy tail. It is often seen scurrying through leaf litter or scampering quickly along the branches of fallen trees. At higher elevations in montane forest, the Mountain Tree Shrew (*Tupaia montana*) is one of the commonest small mammals, especially on Mount Kinabalu and the adjacent Crocker Range. Here, this delightful little creature is regularly encountered and easily observed, although their quick, nervous movements can make them infuriating to try and observe for any extended period. It is active throughout the day and forages mainly on the ground: fruit, insects and other small invertebrates are preferred foods. On the trails leading to the summit of Mount Kinabalu, Mountain Tree Shrews are frequently seen foraging and scavenging around rest spots and picnic sights, and have become habituated and approachable.

Rodents

By far the largest group of small mammals on Borneo (and indeed the world) is the rodents (order Rodentia); worldwide there are around 2000 species, at least 61 of which occur on Borneo. Squirrels (family Sciuridae) are the island's most conspicuous rodents, and these can be divided neatly into two quite different groups: the diurnal ground-dwelling and arboreal tree squirrels, and the nocturnal flying squirrels.

Squirrels

The island's largest arboreal species is the Giant Squirrel (*Ratufa affinis*), which may be up to 80cm (32 inches) in length (including a 40cm/16-inch) tail) and weigh 1.5kg (3½ pounds). It is highly variable in colour; indeed, several distinct subspecies have been proposed, largely based on different coat coloration and pattern. Some forms are very pale honey brown, while others are very dark brown with pale creamy underparts. All of them construct ball-like nests in the highest trees, and rarely descend to lower levels. In stark contrast the Plain Pygmy Squirrel (*Exilisciurus exilis*) weighs a mere 15 to 20g (0.4 to 0.6 ounces). It is a dynamic little animal, constantly scurrying up trunks and along branches, and is capable of surprisingly long leaps between adjacent boughs.

Equally agile are larger species such as Prevost's Squirrel (*Callosciurus prevostii*) and the Plantain Squirrel (*Callosciurus notatus*), both of which are highly active and at times launch themselves from one branch to the next with impressive leaps, sometimes exceeding 5m (16.5 feet) or more. With this in mind it is not difficult to imagine the evolutionary sequence that, step by step, led to the arrival of flying squirrels, a group that has taken leaping between tree trunks to an altogether more spectacular level.

The common feature shared by all flying squirrels is a furred membrane called a patagium that stretches between the fore and rear limbs. When the animal leaps with its limbs outstretched, the extended membrane becomes a parachute that enables flying squirrels to glide considerable distances. In the larger species, such as the Red Giant Flying Squirrel (*Petaurista petaurista*), these glides can exceed 100m (330 feet) or more. However, there is no propulsion, so "flying" involves an animal climbing to the higher levels of a tree before launching itself towards its intended target tree. As it descends, it glides with the ability to steer and manoeuvre moderately by changing limb and tail position. As the squirrel approaches a landing area, it turns its body and tail upwards to slow down and stall the flight, before grasping the trunk with its claws. Not only has this become an economical way of moving through the canopy (see Flying Animals of the Forest, page 30), it is also a very effective way of escaping potential arboreal predators. However, once on a tree trunk, their speed and movements are hindered by the patagium, and they could be easy targets for

LEFT: *The Plantain Squirrel (*Callosciurus notatus) *is commonly found in lowland forests, and at up to around 1600m (5,250 feet) on Mount Kinabalu.*

OPPOSITE: *The Plain Pygmy Squirrel (*Exilisciurus exilis) *feeds by grazing the surface of tree trunks and branches. Its call is a distinctive squeak.*

sharp-eyed birds of prey; hence they have become nocturnal.

The sight of large species such as the Red Giant Flying Squirrel and Thomas's Flying Squirrel (*Aeromys thomasi*) emerging from nest holes and making their first flights of the night across open spaces is one of the more memorable aspects of dusk in the forests of Borneo. Visitors to Sepilok Forest Reserve and Danum Valley in Sabah are regularly treated to such displays.

The diversity of squirrels in Borneo is quite remarkable (there are 34 species), and begs the questions why there are so many, and how they all survive and avoid competition

with one another. Close scrutiny of their habits provides some revealing answers. The first and most obvious division is between diurnal and nocturnal species: 20 are diurnal and 14 nocturnal (all nocturnal species are flying squirrels). The second major separation amongst the diurnal species is that some are primarily terrestrial (five species), while the remaining 15 species are largely arboreal.

However, the separation does not stop there. The lowland dipterocarp forests that cover much of the island (or at least, that did so historically) themselves have a complex structure and are divided into three main layers: the understorey, middle layer and canopy/emergent trees. Different types of squirrel, both diurnal species and nocturnal flying squirrels, show marked preferences to live and forage within these different forest strata, with little cross-over. Further, within each layer, cohabiting species then target different food resources. In this way the forest is compartmentalized into distinct ecological units or niches that are each occupied by a different squirrel species. For instance, the lower forest understorey is the domain of the Red-cheeked Flying Squirrel (*Hylopetes spadiceus*) at night; by day, it is the domain of Low's Squirrel (*Sundasciurus lowii*), which feeds mainly on fruits, insects and fungi, and the Plain Pygmy Squirrel, which grazes the surface of tree bark. On the other hand, the canopy is preferred by Prevost's Squirrel and the Giant Squirrel, the former eating just fruits and nuts, the latter leaves and unripe fruit.

There is further separation with increased altitude, as some species prefer montane regions. For instance, on Mount

Kinabalu, Prevost's Squirrel is quite common at lower and middle elevations, but above 1300m (3,400 feet), it is replaced by the Kinabalu Squirrel (*Callosciurus baluensis*), a locally endemic species restricted to the mountain areas of north-west Sabah.

Porcupines

Borneo is also home to three species of porcupine (family Hystricidae), all confined principally to lowland areas. Both the Common Porcupine (*Hystrix brachyuran*) and Long-tailed Porcupine (*Trichys fasciculata*) also occur in mainland South-East Asia and on Sumatra, while the Thick-spined Porcupine (*Thecurus crassispinis*) is endemic to Borneo.

Rats

The remaining rodents on the island are all less easily observed as they are primarily nocturnal. Most are numerous species of rats and mice, many terrestrial, but some tree-dwelling. While many are broadly distributed around the island, some are very localized; this applies particularly to the handful of species that live only in montane environments, such as the Summit Rat (*Rattus baluensis*), known only from the summit area of Mount Kinabalu, and the Long-tailed Mountain Rat (*Niviventer rapit*), Mountain Spiny Rat (*Maxomys alticola*) and Mountain Giant Rat (*Sundamys infraluteus*) also known from higher elevations on Kinabalu, together with other montane areas like Gunung Trus Madi and Gunung Mulu.

outstretched, they take on a far more graceful air and can execute glides in excess of 70m (230 feet).

To avoid predation by raptors, they are active around dusk and dawn and after nightfall. The day is usually spent resting tight against a tree trunk, or hanging upside down beneath a branch. Their diet consists of leaves, shoots, buds, flowers and sap; their lower incisors are modified into a 'comb', used to scrape and strain sap from trees. A specialized stomach allows them to gain the maximum nutrition from this diet.

Pangolins

Equally unusual, but for very different reasons, is the Malay Pangolin (*Manis javanica*). With an overcoat made of overlapping scales that resembles a terracotta tile roof, no other mammal has such an effective suit of body armour. Body hair is one of the defining characteristics of a mammal, and despite the obvious reptilian appearance, the scales of a pangolin grow from the skin beneath and are in effect hair that has become modified into horn.

Such armour plating serves two main functions: firstly, it makes the animal virtually impregnable to predators when it curls into a tight ball; and secondly, it protects the pangolin from the bites and stings of their main food sources, ants and termites. The gathering of such a specialized diet is further helped by an elongated, probing snout, a long, sticky tongue and thick, gooey saliva that both lubricates and protects. However, pangolins do not have teeth, and have also lost the jaw muscles to chew, so instead, the ants and termites are ground up in a highly modified stomach. While they may forage on the ground much of the time, pangolins are also good climbers, and are capable of raiding nests in the canopy.

This species is found throughout South-East Asia and much of the Indonesian Archipelago, and on Borneo it is known from

Mammal Oddities

Two of the island's mammals are out-and-out curiosities that aptly demonstrate the outlandish inventiveness of evolution. The first is the Colugo (*Cynocephalus variegates*), otherwise rather confusingly called a Flying Lemur; the other is the Pangolin (*Manis javanica*).

The Colugo or Flying Lemur

The Colugo, or Flying Lemur, is neither a true flier (they glide) nor a true lemur; they are primates from the island of Madagascar. There are two Colugo species, both restricted to South-East Asia, and these belong to an order of mammals called the *Dermoptera*, which literally means 'skin wings'.

It is often the unlikely shadowy shape of a Colugo gliding between two trees at dusk that is one's first inkling of the animal. Although they rest on and climb up trunks, so effective is their camouflage against the bark that they are very difficult to spot. Because of the membrane that stretches between their limbs and behind to the tip of the tail, they are cumbersome climbers and tend to move up trunks in clumsy, rabbit-like hops. However, with their wing membranes, or patagium,

sites all over the island in both lowlands and hills, up to around 1700m (5,600 feet) on Mount Kinabalu. However, being solitary and nocturnal, it is not frequently seen.

Throughout much of their range, pangolins are hunted mercilessly for the traditional medicine market; it is believed that their ground-up scales have healing and aphrodisiacal qualities (see Wildlife Trade and Hunting, page 138).

Carnivores

Wherever you may be in the world, carnivores attract attention and stir emotions. Perhaps more than any other group, they are the animals that people want to see, whether it be big cats in East Africa, bears in Alaska or tigers in India. In many ways they are like a precious stone – veiled in secrecy and mystery, where sightings are rare and to be treasured. This is especially

the case in Borneo, where the dense forests and the largely nocturnal lifestyles of most of the island's carnivores make sightings very difficult and highly prized.

Cats

Unlike mainland South-East Asia, where tigers and leopards still roam, the forests of Borneo are not home to any large super-predator. However, what the island's largest feline

might lack in size, it more than makes up for in beauty. That said, the Clouded Leopard (*Neofelis nebulosa*) is not a small animal, being broadly similar to a medium-sized domestic dog: shoulder height 60-75cm (24-29 inches); total length, including tail, 140-180cm (55-70 inches); weight 15-23kg (33-50 pounds). This shy, secretive cat is found in the rainforests throughout mainland South-East Asia and on Sumatra, although it probably reaches its highest densities in Borneo.

Its name is derived from the large, cloud-shaped blotches that cover its flanks; these are edged on one side in dense black, creating a shadow effect, and contrast dramatically with the ochrous-to-brown underlying coat colour. The overall effect creates one of the most beautiful fur patterns of any cat.

In mainland Malaysia, one of the species' local names translates as 'branch-of-tree-tiger', which gives obvious and strong indications to the species' habits. Indeed, the combination of short, powerful legs, broad paws and a long tail are all adaptations that suggest a tree-climbing existence, and it has long been assumed that Clouded Leopards are primarily arboreal hunters; but there have been few observations in the wild to provide confirmation. Recent research is beginning to peel away some of the layers of mystery, and with one or two surprises. That they are skilled climbers is in little doubt; however, it now seems they are far more terrestrial and even diurnal in activity than was previously thought. Although animals regularly climb trees to rest in, most movement and hunting is on the ground. Further, primates were thought to be regular prey, but while

ABOVE: *An adaptable animal, The Common Palm Civet* (Paradoxurus hermaphroditus) *forages on the ground and in trees.*

BELOW: *The Clouded Leopard (*Neofelis nebulosa) *is shy and infrequently seen. Photographs like this one are exceedingly rare.*

ABOVE: *The Binturong (Arctictis binturong) is an agile climber, capable of climbing the tallest trees to feed on fruit.*

Clouded Leopards do ambush monkeys, and even gibbons from time to time, most of their prey is taken on the ground. They are capable of tackling large species such as Sambar and Bearded Pigs, although smaller species of mammal, such as mouse deer and birds, are frequently eaten. Indeed, in areas along some forest edges, rats appear to constitute up to half of their diet.

Borneo's forests are also home to four other species of small cat, all equally elusive and ghost-like. Of these, only the Bay Cat (*Catopuma badia*), notable for its rich chestnut-red coat colour (although some animals are grey), is endemic to the island. In fact, the species remains largely unknown, and has been seen only infrequently, mainly in areas of highland forest, and also in some lower-lying areas such as Danum Valley.

The Marbled Cat (*Pardofelis marmorata*), Flat-headed Cat (*Prionailurus planiceps*) and Leopard Cat (*Prionailurus bengalensis*) are all found in mainland South-East Asia and Sumatra, as well as in Borneo. All are nocturnal hunters that prefer to pursue their prey on the ground, although they are capable of climbing. The Leopard Cat is one of the smallest

wild-cat species in the world (it is about the size of a small domestic cat), and is also more adaptable than the other species. Ochre-yellow to golden-brown, and beautifully spotted like a miniature Leopard, this diminutive feline has adapted well to forest edges, plantations and even the periphery of villages and towns. This is probably because these areas support larger numbers of rodents than pristine forest. One advantage as a result of this is that the Leopard Cat is seen more often than other cats on the island.

Other Carnivores

The majority of the island's other carnivores belongs to one of three groups: the civets (family Viverridae), the weasels and their kin (family Mustelidae), and the mongooses (family Herpestidae). Like the cats, these are difficult animals to see.

Civets

One of the most unusual civit is the Binturong (*Arctictis binturong*), sometimes also called a 'bear-cat', which is erroneous as it is neither a bear nor a cat. It is, in fact, a type of viverrid, a diverse group of carnivores that includes the genets, civets and linsangs. The Binturong is certainly an atypical member of the family: it is large and rather heavy-

bodied, with thick, shaggy, grizzled grey-black fur, prominent ear-tufts and piercing, bead-like red-brown eyes. Belying its rather cumbersome appearance, the Binturong is an adept climber (as are most civets and genets), and is almost totally arboreal. It is unique amongst viverrids in having a prehensile tail, which it uses to excellent effect when moving around the outermost branches of the canopy with surprising agility.

In common with other civets and genets, the Binturong's diet is varied, and includes small vertebrates and invertebrates, although it is principally a fruit eater, preferring ripe fruits, especially figs. If a large fig is fruiting in the forest, it is not uncommon to find a Binturong high in the canopy gorging itself, together with various primates such as gibbons and even Orang-utans.

Other viverrids on Borneo are small, generalist carnivores that feed on both small animals and fruits. The majority are good climbers; some have beautiful coat patterns and markings; and many spend the day asleep in tree holes before emerging to forage after dark. This includes species such as the Common Palm Civet (*Paradoxurus hermaphroditus*) and the Masked Palm Civet (*Paguma larvata*) that often enter plantations and gardens to feed; and also more specialized forest dwellers, such as the Banded Palm Civet (*Hemigalus derbyanus*) and the Banded Linsang (*Prionodon linsang*).

ABOVE: *Being another generalist, the Masked Palm Civet (*Paguma larvata*) lives in both primary and secondary forest. Its varied diet includes small vertebrates, invertebrates and fruit.*

BELOW: *The Malay Badger, or Teledu (*Mydaus javanensis*), is nocturnal, and sleeps in underground burrows. Its presence can often be detected by its strong pervading odour, which is secreted from an anal gland.*

Far more terrestrial in its habits is the Malay Civet or Tangalung (Viverra tangalunga), a species slightly larger than most, which is also nocturnal but rarely climbs trees. It is widespread throughout Borneo and other parts of South-East Asia, and is also very adaptable, not only living within forest, but also the periphery, cultivated areas and gardens. It has even been known to enter forest camps, to scavenge scraps.

The Mongooses

Closely related to the civets are the mongooses (family Herpestidae), another family widespread throughout the Old World tropics. Famous for their snake-catching skills, and immortalized in Rudyard Kipling's *Jungle Book*, mongooses are quite diverse. While some species in Africa or India do prey on snakes and other reptiles and live in open habitats, often in colonies (best known are Meerkats and Banded Mongooses), those in Borneo are solitary forest dwellers, about

BELOW: *The Oriental Short-clawed Otter (*Aonyx cinerea*) is found along a variety of waterways, including estuaries, rivers, streams and lakes, where it feeds on fish, molluscs and crustaceans. It is gregarious and is normally seen in groups, but lone individuals may be encountered. This animal was photographed on the Menanggol River in Sabah.*

which very little is known. There are just two species: the Short-tailed Mongoose (*Herpestes brachyurus*) and the Collared Mongoose (*Herpestes semitorquatus*); both are probably mainly terrestrial and diurnal in their habits.

Mustelids

The weasels and their kin (family Mustelidae) are a very diverse group that tends to be more associated with colder temperate climates than hot equatorial ones. The family not only includes the weasels, but also other familiar groups such as the badgers, otters and martens. Species such as the Yellow-throated Marten (*Martes flavigula*) and Malay or Barefoot Weasel (*Mustela nudiceps*) are widespread throughout South-East Asia and the islands of Sumatra and Borneo. Both species are terrestrial and arboreal, and prey on small mammals, birds, reptiles and frogs. The Malay Weasel is a striking animal, not least because of its bright orange coat colour and white head.

In contrast, the curious Ferret-Badger (*Melogale everetti*) is endemic; it appears to be restricted to the higher elevations of Mount Kinabalu up to around 3000m (10,000 feet), and possibly Mount Tambayukon to the north of Kinabalu. A high proportion of its diet is possibly earthworms.

The playful and inquisitive nature of otters makes them perennial favourites. Although three species are found on the

island, the Oriental Short-clawed Otter (*Aonyx cinerea*) is far more likely to be seen than the others. Unlike other otters, this species virtually lacks all webbing between its toes and has short, blunt claws. Nevertheless, its hands are extremely sensitive and dextrous, and it is able to grip and manipulate prey such as crabs and molluscs with ease. It is found throughout the island in both coastal areas and by rivers and lakes, and often in groups of eight or more. In coastal mangroves it may be seen at low tide foraging over the exposed mud, and it often stands up on its hind legs to investigate its immediate surroundings.

Sun Bear

Borneo's largest carnivore is the Sun Bear (*Helarctos malayanus*), although it is actually the smallest of the world's bears (family Ursidae): adults stand around 70cm (28 inches) at the shoulder, and weigh up to 65kg (143 pounds). It is a curious animal, with a short, black coat that derives its name

(both common and generic) from the ochre or white circular marking on the upper chest, which is thought to look like the sun (*Hele* is Greek for 'heat of the sun', *arktos* is Greek for bear) – although this marking is variable and can be faint, and is often shaped more like a 'V' or 'C'.

Sun Bears are primarily nocturnal (although males are sometimes diurnal), and largely tree-dwelling, constructing nests from small branches in which to sleep during the day. These nests are similar to those built by Orang-utans, but tend to be located much closer to the trunk and are less skilfully woven. Like most bears, they are omnivorous; recent studies in Danum Valley suggest termites, beetles and beetle larvae make up a significant part of the diet, together with large amounts of fruit, especially figs (*Ficus* sp.). Insect feeding sites correlate to decaying wood and tree cavities, and bees nest are also important. When feeding on insects, Sun Bears use their strong forepaws to tear open rotten logs and nests, and lick out the insects with a very long, sticky tongue. In human-populated areas, rubbish and agricultural fruit are also eaten.

Sun bears are active year-round (unlike other bears, they do not hibernate), and are not seasonal breeders. On mainland South-East Asia there is an unfortunate trend to keep young animals as pets, but once the animal becomes adult it is generally too unruly and unpredictable. In Borneo, this is one of very few animals that is potentially dangerous, and if encountered should be treated with caution.

Larger Mammals (Ungulates)

Although it no longer has any formal taxonomic meaning, 'ungulate' remains a convenient umbrella term that refers to hoofed, grazing mammals. With the exception of the Sumatran Rhinoceros, all ungulates resident on Borneo are terrestrial, even-toed (order Artiodactyla), and have two functional hoofed toes and two reduced 'dew toes' on each foot. The ungulate fauna of Borneo is impoverished by comparison with other, similar regions of the world, and even those species present tend to occur at rather low densities. This suggests that Borneo's forests do not contain suitable plant species that ruminating browsers find palatable.

LEFT: *The Sun Bear (*Helarctos malayanus*) is the largest terrestrial carnivore on Borneo. The majority of its diet consists of insects and fruit.*

OPPOSITE LEFT: *Although they are large and formidable animals, Bearded Pigs (*Sus barbatus*) are shy and difficult to see.*

OPPOSITE RIGHT: *The larger of the two mouse deer in Borneo, the Greater Mouse Deer (*Tragulus napu*) inhabits tall primary forests.*

Wild Cattle

Only one species of wild cattle occurs on Borneo: the Tembadau or Banteng (*Bos javanicus*). While broadly similar in appearance to the wild cattle of India, the Gaur (*Bos gaurus*), the Tembadau is considerably smaller: males are larger than females and can reach around 1.6m (5.2 feet) at the shoulder. They are forest animals and strictly nocturnal, almost certainly a consequence of past hunting pressure, and are very shy wherever they still occur. Their range has certainly been drastically reduced, and today they are found only in the drainage basins of major rivers in Eastern Sabah, like the Kinabatangan, Segama, Tabin and upper Padas and some isolated and scattered parts of south and central Kalimantan.

Pigs

Even if the animals themselves are not seen, evidence of Bearded Pigs (*Sus barbatus*) – namely their destructive diggings and droppings – is regularly encountered on walks in most forest areas. Like most wild pigs, their foraging technique is uncompromising as earth is moved and roots and tubers excavated, and this habit certainly makes them very unpopular visitors to cocoa and palm plantations. Overall, their diet is extremely varied, and includes all types of vegetable matter (fruits, seeds, leaves, shoots and roots and so on), earthworms, other invertebrates and small vertebrates such as frogs, lizards and young birds.

They are large animals, big males reaching close to 1m (3.2 feet) at the shoulder and weighing up to 100kg (220 pounds). Only adult males develop the luxuriant long-haired beard around the entire muzzle. Bearded Pigs generally live in small groups, but occasionally will amalgamate into much larger herds that travel and forage widely. They are adept swimmers, and rivers are no barrier to their movements. Adult females make nests of shrubs and saplings in areas where flooding is unlikely – generally higher ground and ridge-tops – and give birth to litters of up to 11 young.

also active during the day). Sambar are shy, solitary animals that are rarely seen, although it may be that such behaviour is due to heavy human hunting pressure. There are also records of the similar-sized Javan Rusa Deer (*Cervus timorensis*) from areas in southern Kalimantan. These animals were almost certainly introduced during the 17th century, but have probably now been exterminated.

The only deer endemic to the island is the Bornean Yellow Muntjac (*Muntiacus atherodes*); it is widespread in most forest areas, although there appears to be a preference for coastal forests and lower elevations of hill forest. In more hilly and mountainous areas, evidence suggests its close relative, the Red or Indian Muntjac (*Muntiacus muntjak*), is more common. Muntjacs are renowned for their piercing single note alarm call, which gives rise to their alternative common name of 'barking deer'.

The Sumatran Rhinoceros

Borneo's rarest large animal is without question the Sumatran or Asian Two-Horned Rhinoceros (*Dicerorhinus sumatrensis*). Of the three species of rhino that live in various parts of Asia, it is the only one with two horns. Weighing 500-800 kg (0.5-0.8 tonnes), it is the smallest living rhino, and also the only species with obvious shaggy hair, sometimes leading to it being called the Hairy Rhinoceros. As is often the case with scientific names, its generic name *Dicerorhinus* carries meaning: it is from the Greek *di* meaning 'two', *cero* meaning 'horn', and *rhinus* meaning 'nose'. The species name *sumatrensis* more obviously refers to the locality from where it was initially described.

The Sumatran Rhino is reddish-brown in colour, with variable amounts of hair – some sparse, some dense – over its head and body. The hair tends to be much shorter in wild animals than in those in captivity, because of abrasion from forest vegetation. The ears are always fringed, and there is heavy wrinkling around the eyes. The animal's front horn may reach 70cm (28 inches) in length, although this is exceptional; 20-35cm (8-14 inches) is normal. The rear horn is always considerably shorter, and is generally less than 15cm (6 inches) in length. The horn is not a weapon, but instead is used to help dig wallows and pull down vegetation. Calves are particularly hirsute, being born with a characteristic dense covering of black hair, which gradually turns reddish-brown as the animal matures.

Two subspecies are recognized: the western race, Dicerorhinus sumatrensis sumatrensis, is found on Sumatra and Peninsular Malaysia, while the eastern race, Dicerorhinus

Mouse Deer

Chevrotains or mouse deer (family Tragulidae) are the smallest ruminants. In all, there are only four species, two of which are found on Borneo. The most diminutive is the Lesser Mouse Deer (*Tragulus javanicus*), which at a mere 2kg (4.4 pounds) in weight is little bigger than a large rabbit. At between 4 and 5kg (9 and 11 pounds), the Greater Mouse Deer (*Tragulus napu*) is twice the size of its smaller cousin. Both are nocturnal forest dwellers characterized by rather rounded hog-like bodies and very thin legs, and are largely solitary creatures that feed mainly on fallen fruits. Unlike many other ruminants, they do not have horns or antlers; instead, the males develop 'tusks' – long upper canines that protrude below the upper lip and outside the lower jaw – which are their primary weapon when fighting other males. Being small, they are regularly preyed upon by large snakes such as the Reticulated Python, and also by the Clouded Leopard.

Deer

True deer (family Cervidae) also occur on Borneo. The largest is the Sambar (*Cervus unicolor*), which in Borneo at least is largely nocturnal (those in the more open forests of India are sumatrensis harrissoni, is confined to Borneo. At the beginning of the 20th century, this animal was widespread and reasonably common throughout the island, but since that time there has been a catastrophic decline in numbers.

While numerically the Sumatran Rhino may not be the rarest of the world's five species of rhino – that dubious accolade belongs to the Javan Rhino (*Rhinoceros sondaicus*) – there is little doubt that it is the most endangered. Even the most optimistic estimates suggest there are no more than around 300 individuals, and these are scattered in highly fragmented populations in parts of mainland Malaysia, Sumatra and Borneo; it is unlikely that any single population contains more than 60 animals, and with many much smaller than this, their long-term viability is highly questionable.

Poaching is the major culprit for the species decline. This is done principally to supply the demand for horn and body parts that have been used in traditional medicines in parts of South-

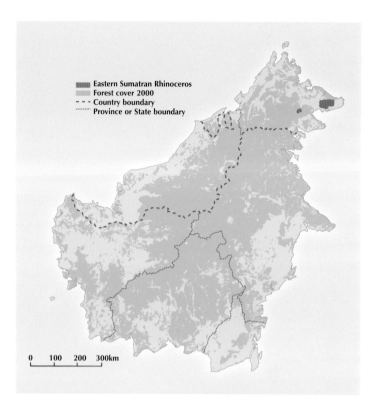

BELOW: *Conservation efforts for the Sumatran Rhinoceros (*Dicerorhinus sumatrensis*) concentrate on the preservation of habitat and eradication of poaching.*

East Asia for centuries (rhino-horn trade between Borneo and China has been recorded more than 2,000 years ago). Historically, these products were regarded as the sole preserve of the rich, but the 1970s saw a leap in prosperity throughout many Asian communities, and this fuelled a massive increase in demand for rhino and other animal products (*see* Wildlife Trade and Hunting, page 138). Throughout their range, it is thought Sumatran Rhino numbers have suffered a 50 per cent reduction in the last 10 to 15 years.

In Borneo, there may be no more than 40 animals left, scattered in remote corners in the north-east of Sabah, most notably Danum Valley and Tabin; there are almost certainly none remaining in either Kalimantan or Sarawak. The largest single sub-population is in Tabin Wildlife Reserve, where there are thought to be around 25 animals. It is here that the Sabah Wildlife Department and various overseas conservation agencies are concentrating their efforts.

Unlike rhino poaching in Africa or India, the dense forest habitat means that hunting with guns is ineffective, so instead, poachers set indiscriminate pit-fall traps and snares, and this often results in a rhino suffering a long, agonizing death before the poacher returns to remove its horn.

With the support of non-governmental organizations like WWF, SOS Rhino and Save the Rhino International, the Sabah authorities have established a field team to monitor and help protect wild rhinos at Tabin and in the Sabah Foundation forest concession. It is hoped that more funding will allow further teams to maintain a permanent presence in these areas to

ABOVE: *Populations of the Sumatran Rhinoceros (Dicerorhinus sumatrensis) on Borneo are now restricted to the extreme north east of the island, and are centred on Danum Valley and the Tabin Wildlife Reserve.*

OPPOSITE: *Like all elephants, Bornean Pygmy Elephants (Elephas maximus 'borneensis') eat a huge amount of foliage each day. The variety of species they browse is considerable, but they do spend a lot of time close to rivers feeding on reeds, bathing and drinking.*

safeguard the remaining rhinos.

A debate still exists over whether protection of wild rhinos or captive breeding will provide the better route to saving this extremely endangered species. Most of the Sumatran rhinos brought into captivity since 1987 have died without breeding, thus giving renewed urgency to protective measures for wild rhinos. Yet encouragement comes from halfway around the world at the Cinncinnati Zoo where in 2001 a female Sumatran Rhino, 'Emi', gave birth to a male calf 'Andalas', who became the first of his species born in captivity for 112 years. In 2004, Emi produced a second calf, this time a female.

Behaviour and Habitat
While the sight of a rhino may be poor, its senses of smell and hearing are very good, and serve it well in dense forest environments. They are a solitary species with a very large range: adults regularly scent-mark scrapes and saplings with faeces and urine to reinforce their occupancy of an area. This

correspondingly means they always live at low densities, so the problem of individuals finding a mate is further compounded today by their extremely low numbers. While conflicts between individuals are rare, they are capable of inflicting deep wounds with long, dagger-shaped lower incisors.

Their lifespan is thought to be similar to that of other rhinos, around 35 to 40 years, but they probably do not reach sexual maturity until at least seven years in females and ten years in males. Not surprisingly, they are also slow breeders, with females only able to produce a calf once every four to five years.

The Sumatran Rhino is primarily a browser, using its prehensile upper lip to grasp leaves and some fallen fruits. Its feeding habits may provide a clue to its apparent sensitivity to habitat degradation and change. Their preferred habitat is pristine lowland and middle altitude tropical forest, where ideally there are mineral licks and suitable areas in which to wallow. Even when adjacent to large tracts of primary forest, apparently good areas of secondary forest do not appear to suit rhinos. This may be because secondary forest tends to have a very dense, often impenetrable understorey and a reduced shrub layer at the rhino's preferred browsing height.

Rhinos spend time wallowing every day, often returning time after time to favourite mud holes. These may begin as temporary pools, but are maintained and deepened by digging

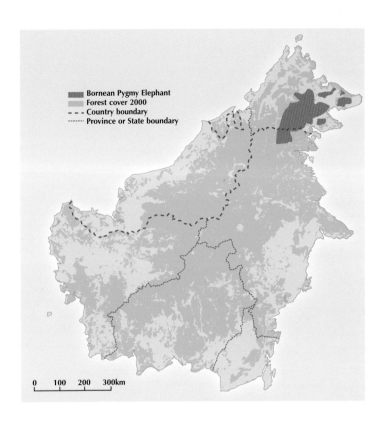

with the feet and horn. Regular mud bathing is essential for maintaining skin condition, thermo-regulation and to rid themselves of skin parasites.

ELEPHANTS AND HUMANS

Perhaps the Bornean Pygmy Elephant's most peculiar feature is its tameness. No one of sound mind would ever dream of approaching a wild Asian or African Elephant closely on foot, yet the elephants of Borneo show a remarkable level of tolerance that is as beguiling as it is endearing. Quite why this should be is also a matter of conjecture.

Anyone visiting the Lower Kinabatangan Wildlife Sanctuary has an excellent chance of experiencing this behaviour first hand, as elephant sightings are becoming an increasingly regular occurrence. During boat trips along the main Kinabatangan river and its tributary, the Menanggol river, small herds can often be seen when they come down to the river's edge to feed and drink. Their placid temperament allows boats to approach quite closely, and providing one remains quiet, a long, enjoyable and fulfilling encounter is possible. (The onset of too many tourists can, however, inhibit elephants crossing rivers, and potentially cause stress, hindering movement to new feeding sites). Even individual elephants that get upset when they are disturbed behave in a surprising way. In a similar fashion to other elephants, they may trumpet their displeasure and carry out mock charges, but following this display, they turn turtle, show their backsides to the party responsible, and perform a curious rear-end shuffle!

The Bornean Pygmy Elephant

The origin of elephants in Borneo has long been a contentious issue, endlessly debated by zoologists and conservationists working in the region. For a long time the majority view seemed to be that elephants were an introduced species, probably descended from stock brought from mainland South-East Asia or Sumatra, and presented as gifts by the British East India Company to the Sultan of Sulu in 1750. It is then supposed that these semi-domesticated, tame elephants were released (either accidentally or deliberately) into the forests of north-east Borneo, and subsequently became feral, breeding and expanding their population to around 2,000 by the early 20th century. Consequently, these animals have been assigned a low priority in terms of their conservation status, and have been assumed to be artificial extensions of the range of either

ABOVE LEFT: *Like other elephants in Asia, only male Bornean Pygmy Elephants (*Elephas maximus 'borneensis'*) have tusks.*

OPPOSITE: *Despite their large size, Bornean Pygmy Elephants can move with surprising stealth. This female approached to within 10m (33 feet) of the photographer. Sensing no danger, she paid him little attention.*

the Asian Elephant (*Elephas maximus indicus*), or more likely the Sumatra subspecies, *Elephas maximus sumatrensis*.

The alternative theory is that they do indeed represent an indigenous population that warrants a separate identity and differentiation from elephant populations elsewhere in South-East Asia. Outwardly there are certainly traits and characteristics that make Borneo's elephants different. Most

during the Pleistocene era, when sea levels fluctuated dramatically with the advance and retreat of vast ice sheets, elephants were able to walk across land bridges. Indeed, during times when sea levels were at their lowest, the Malay Peninsula, Sumatra, Java, Borneo and Bali formed one landmass known as Sundaland. Once elephants had spread across to some of these areas, subsequent rises in water levels, the last of which was around 18,000 years ago, effectively marooned separate populations on the mainland, Sumatra and Borneo. However, historically on Borneo there is no evidence for elephant populations anywhere other than the north-east corner of the island, where they survive today, which certainly adds to the mystery of their arrival and isolation. A further mystery is the existence of the bones – now in Muzium Lambung Mangkurat, South Kalimantan – of a very large elephant dug from a swamp west of Banjamasin.

While this evidence has revealed the distinct nature and evolution of Borneo's elephants, their exact taxonomic status has yet to be determined. Some have been quick to propose an endemic subspecies, the Bornean Pygmy Elephant (*Elephas maximus 'borneensis'*), while others have adopted a more cautious approach until research is finalized. Whatever conclusions are eventually drawn, it now seems certain that Borneo's elephants represent a distinct population that has been evolving in splendid isolation for a considerable period of time, and as such, warrants special attention from wildlife departments and conservation agencies.

As their name implies, Bornean Pygmy Elephants are small, indeed they are the smallest of all elephants: males rarely exceed 2.5m (8.2 feet) in height (measured to the top of the head), while a big female measures around 2m (6.6 feet). Even large males probably weigh little more than 3000 kg (3 tonnes), and females around 2200 kg (2.2 tonnes). By way of comparison, male mainland Asian Elephants regularly stand more than 3m (10 feet) tall and weigh up to 5.5 tonnes. Other peculiarities include long tails (perhaps to help swish away flies) and straight tusks (only possessed by males). It is quite probable that these features, together with their relatively small size, are adaptations to their dense forest environment (straight tusks are a feature they share with forest elephants in Africa).

Today (and historically), Borneo's elephants are confined to areas in the north-east of the island, primarily in Sabah and also just into the north-east corner of Kalimantan. It may be that this reflects a correlation with areas high in natural minerals, where soils are most fertile. Bornean Elephants are found in lowland dipterocarp and riverine forest, and occasionally enter swamp and nipah forest to forage. They also venture into plantations

obviously, they are smaller than their counterparts on the mainland, and they also have more rounded bodies, relatively larger ears and longer tails, and rather straight tusks. Interestingly, these differences show considerable similarity to the differences that separate the Central and West African Forest Elephant (*Loxodonta cyclotis*) from the larger, more widespread and familiar Savanna Elephant (*Loxodonta africana*) of the African Plains.

Genetic analysis has revealed some startling findings that confirm that Borneo's elephants are distinct from other elephants in Asia, and that they have been ploughing their own evolutionary furrow for at least the past 18,000 years, possibly as long as 300,000 years. Evidence suggests that Asian elephants split into two main lineages some three million years ago, with the smaller of these offshoots comprising the elephants now found in the Malay Peninsula and on Sumatra and Borneo. Further, it seems that Bornean elephants themselves may have diverged from this lineage around 300,000 years ago, although it is difficult to pinpoint when they actually colonized Borneo. One possibility is that (coconut, cocoa and palm oil), and into gardens where they raid crops and cause considerable damage.

A Conservation Issue

The recent establishment of the Bornean Pygmy Elephant as a distinct lineage has dramatically elevated their importance in conservation terms, because they constitute what is termed an 'evolutionary significant unit'. This has happened at a time when shrinking available habitat is bringing them into conflict more and more with humans.

Current estimates suggest the total number of elephants in Borneo is around 1,600, and that these are concentrated in an area stretching from Sebuku Sembakung in north-east Kalimantan, through to Maliau, Danum, Deramakot, Kinabatangan and Tabin on the eastern side of Sabah. The Lower Kinabatangan Wildlife Sanctuary holds one of the largest single populations (perhaps 150 to 200 elephants), and regular interaction with the people of the area highlights the problem.

The Lower Kinabatangan is now a mosaic of fragmented forest blocks and narrow interlinking corridors following the course of the river, which is surrounded primarily by oil-palm plantations and local villages, where crops such as bananas, tapioca, papaya and sweet potatoes are grown. Crucially, huge areas were turned over to oil-palm plantations before the value of the Kinabatangan was realized, and appropriate planning and land management was implemented. This has resulted in not only heavy forest fragmentation, but also the blocking of traditional elephant migration routes. This now means that the elephants pass through plantations where they feed on young palms and are, therefore, harried and persecuted by plantation owners. Further, they raid crops adjacent to local villages and are again encouraged to move on, often with the use of fire crackers.

Even worse, there have been instances of direct persecution. Snares have been responsible for causing horrific injuries to some individuals, and there have also been reports of local people killing elephants for their ivory, skin and meat in the Lower Kinabatangan and Tabin Wildlife Sanctuary.

Such persecution is forcing the elephants into smaller areas and increasingly narrow corridors, where they become concentrated. In the past, herds of more than 15 animals were uncommon, as populations were dispersed throughout larger areas of forest. Today, gatherings exceeding 60 elephants are encountered with increasing regularity in parts of the Lower Kinabatangan, particularly along the banks of the main river and major tributaries, indicating the shrinking options they have to roam over larger areas.

The Lower Kinabatangan Wildlife Sanctuary, which was gazetted in 1999 and pledged by the Malaysian Government as its 'Gift to the Earth', currently covers an area of 26,000ha (64,250 acres). However, recent estimates suggest plantations

TOP: *A curious aspect of Bornean Pygmy Elephants (*Elephas maximus 'borneensis'*) is their apparent tolerance of humans.*

BOTTOM: *Shrinking ranges bring Bornean Pygmy Elephants and humans into conflict. The festering wounds of this female are the result of a snare. She was tranquilized, treated and later released.*

are still expanding and forest clearance is continuing: between 2000 and 2005, perhaps 20 per cent of remaining forests in the area have gone. Obviously, if this trend continues, the impact on the Bornean Pygmy Elephant populations will be potentially disastrous, and will further increase levels of conflict between remaining elephants and the people of the area. To try and better understand the movements and migration patterns of the elephants in the region, staff from the Sabah Wildlife Department and WWF's Asian Rhino and Elephant Strategy (AREAS) have now radio-collared some individuals, and are able to track their movements via satellite. It is hoped that this work will identify those remaining forest areas that are critical to the elephants, so that they can be preserved at all costs.

Primates

The forests of Borneo are home to some of the world's most interesting and unusual primates, ranging in size from the Orang-utan, weighing up to 100kg (220 pounds), to the Western Tarsier, weighing a diminutive 120g (4.2 ounces). Dense forests are notorious for making wildlife viewing difficult, and in some places tracking down primates can be a time-consuming and exhausting business. This is not necessarily the case in Borneo, however, as some of the island's prime locations are amongst the best places to see a variety of primate species with relative ease.

In total, the island has 13 primates: two small nocturnal species, five species of leaf monkey or langur, the Proboscis Monkey, two species of macaque and three species of ape. Most are found throughout lowland forest, and some into the lower elevations of montane forest. Species such as the Proboscis Monkey have become specialized and are able to survive in habitats such as mangrove and swamp forest that most other primates find unsuitable.

LEFT: *The young of Silvered Leaf Monkeys (*Trachypithecus cristata*) are often bright orange, although there is considerable variation across their range that correlates to subtle taxonomic differences.*

BELOW: *Dominant male Pig-tailed Macaques (*Macaca nemestrina*) are physically strong, and can be aggressive and intimidating.*

Monkeys

Monkeys are the most conspicuous and gregarious primates on the island. An island historically covered in different types of forest is tailor-made for their various ways of life, and eons of evolution have moulded an impressive diversity.

Broadly speaking, Old World monkeys (family Cercopithecidae) fall into two groups. The typical monkeys (subfamily Cercopithecinae) are gregarious generalists that are widespread in both Africa and Asia. On Borneo, they are represented by the macaques, a genus widespread in Central and South-East Asia. On the other hand, the Colobus and Leaf Monkeys (subfamily Colobinae) are more specialized, and as a group have their stronghold in Asia. The Asian odd-nosed monkeys are also Colobines, although they cannot strictly be described as either a colobus or leaf monkey.

The Macaques

If ever a species epitomized the anthropomorphic 'cheeky monkey', it is the Long-tailed Macaque (*Macaca fascicularis*): social, inquisitive and mischievous, these highly adaptable animals thrive in a variety of habitats. They are equally at home plucking buds and leaves from the highest branches, sifting meticulously through the detritus deposited by high tides in coastal mangroves, or raiding with lightning speed the unguarded dining room of a forest lodge. Indeed, they are particularly fond of forests along the banks of rivers and coastal areas, and often spend long periods of time foraging in the margins. Their diet regularly includes invertebrates and small vertebrates, including crustaceans and molluscs, and for this reason they are also known as Crab-eating Macaques.

Much larger in stature is the Pig-tailed Macaque (*Macaca nemestrina*), another species equally at home on the ground as well as in the trees. These are imposing monkeys with impressive physiques, and often appear more menacing than mischievous. Large, strutting males have a furrow-browed, thuggish quality that is comparable to all the charm of a rugby front-row forward. Their body language – teeth bearing and eye-brow flashing – sends out a clear message, 'Don't mess with me!'

Both macaque species live in large troops with complex social hierarchies, where group dynamics and politics are a constant feature of daily life. It is not surprising, therefore, that posturing, display, aggression and submission are obvious and omnipresent elements in their behavioural repertoire.

Leaf Monkeys

Far more gracile and appealing in their demeanour are the Leaf Monkeys, or langurs. These species are exclusively tree-dwelling and feed predominantly on leaves and seeds of

ABOVE: *The Maroon Sureli or Red Leaf Monkey (*Presbytis rubicunda*) is a striking primate that is widely distributed through the lowland forest areas of the island. This animal was photographed in Danum Valley, Sabah.*

legumes. Their most distinctive feature is an unusual stomach – it is partitioned into sacs – that allows them to digest their fibre- and toxin-rich diet more efficiently than other primates.

In all there are five species on the island, although the extent of their various distributions is complex and intriguing. The Banded Leaf Monkey (*Presbytis melalophis*) is found only in restricted lowland western parts of the island, while Hose's Sureli or the Grey Leaf Monkey (*Presbytis hosei*) appears to be restricted to regions principally in the north-west. The Maroon Sureli or Red Leaf Monkey (*Presbytis rubicunda*) prefers lowland areas, and has been found over most of the island, with the exception of the western parts of Sarawak and Central Kalimantan. The White-fronted Sureli (*Presbytis frontata*), so named because of the white spot in the centre of the forehead, is endemic to the island and seems restricted to the centre and south-east. Finally, the Silvered Leaf Monkey (*Trachypithecus cristata*) has been recorded from many coastal areas around the island, and often penetrates inland along major rivers.

ABOVE: *The Silvered Leaf Monkey (*Trachypithecus cristata*) is a highly variable species. This very pale individual belonged to a troop of more regular dark grey animals.*

The Proboscis Monkey

Few primates are as bizarre or charismatic as the Proboscis Monkey (*Nasalis larvatus*). They are adept at making an indelible first impression, although some regard them as grotesque, and others endearing. Early travellers described their appearance variously as 'ludicrous' and 'ridiculous'.

The Proboscis Monkey is the largest of the colobines on the island; males weigh as much as 23kg (50 pounds), while females generally weigh around half this. The monkey's anatomy suggests it is a ground-dweller (they do forage on tidal mudflats in mangroves and the forest floor periodically), although it has effectively become trapped by island climate change in the mangrove and riparian forest it inhabits.

Other than its large size, two features make this an unmistakable species: firstly, its bizarre pendulous nose, and secondly, its outrageous pot belly. These are characteristics largely associated with males, and are not as well developed in females. In fact, their stomachs are relatively twice the size as those of any other Colobine, which means that both male and female Proboscis Monkeys look permanently pregnant. Such features have given rise to one of their less flattering names, *Orang Belanda* or 'Dutchman', since these monkeys reminded the native people of Borneo of the early European explorers. Indeed, *Orang Belanda* remains the most widely used name for the species in Sarawak; in other parts of Borneo they have numerous names, including *Raseng, Rasong, Pika, Bentangan, Bekantan* and *Bangketan*.

The Colobines are principally leaf-eaters, a trait that has established them as the most successful primates in the tropical rainforests of the Old World. Being so heavily reliant on leaves, they have evolved a digestive system that allows them to extract the maximum amount of nutrition from this restricted diet. This has effectively produced a specialized multi-chambered stomach, similar to that of an ungulate, which contains a cocktail of bacteria that helps ferment and digest the foliage. Multi-chambered stomachs require big bellies to accommodate them, and indeed, this is taken to the extreme in the Proboscis Monkey.

There has been much debate as to the function of the nose. Some have suggested it acts like a snorkel when the animals are swimming, but this doesn't explain why males have much larger noses than females. Another theory is that it helps regulate body temperature, but again, this doesn't necessarily explain the discrepancy in nose size between the sexes. The most likely explanation is that the size difference is a result of sexual selection, whereby females prefer males with bigger noses, so big-nosed males monopolize mating with females and therefore produce more offspring than smaller-nosed males. This then results in genes for bigger noses becoming predominant within the population and being passed on to

These distribution patterns are far from fully understood, and may have been altered and compromised by habitat alteration and deforestation that has occurred in many parts of their ranges. However, it seems plausible that in some instances, major rivers have acted as barriers, separating the distributions of different species on either bank.

One curious feature of this monkey is that, in some instances, the young are dramatically different in colour from the adult. For example, adult Red Leaf Monkeys are various shades of chestnut red (similar in colour to an Orang-utan), but their young are creamy white. The most extreme case is the Silvered Leaf Monkey: adults are dark, grizzled metallic grey, while their young are a ridiculously bright orange colour (although there is notable variation, as the infant's colour reflects distinct taxonomic groupings). It is thought that this variation in colour exists in order to attract the mother's sisters and cousins so that they may help protect and rear the babies. After three months or so, the coat colour reverts to the same shade as the adult.

future generations. It is also likely that the large pendulous nose of males acts as a resonating organ and so enhances their vocal range and efficiency.

One other feature makes Proboscis Monkeys unusual: they have partially webbed back feet, something unique amongst primates. Their forest homes are criss-crossed with waterways and river channels. Where these are narrow, they are able to leap spectacularly across, often spanning distances in excess of 10m (33 feet). However, rivers are often much wider, and to cross these they have become adept swimmers. Sometimes they leap part-way across and splash down into the water before swimming the remainder; at other times they enter the water on foot, walking across with their arms held aloft until the water becomes too deep and they are forced to swim in a doggy-paddle fashion. They have also been seen to slide quietly into the water and swim across in Indian-file, with no noise and no splashing. It is thought this is to avoid attracting the attention of crocodiles, their main predator.

This species lives in groups that range in size from three to over 30. They are not territorial, and the home ranges of

ABOVE: *An alpha male Proboscis Monkey (Nasalis larvatus) appears imposing; they can weigh over 20kg (44 pounds).*

BELOW: *During courtship there is considerable posturing and vocalisation between male and female Proboscis Monkeys (Nasalis larvatus).*

ABOVE: *The attention of this troop of Proboscis Monkeys (*Nasalis larvatus*) was grabbed by a large Reticulated Python beneath them.*

LEFT: *Male Proboscis Monkeys can be extremely vocal. This male is shouting at a neighbouring troop on the opposite side of the river.*

OPPOSITE: *Bornean Gibbons (*Hylobates muelleri*) live in close family units and often indulge in extended bouts of acrobatic play.*

neighbouring groups, each up to 9 square kilometres (3.5 square miles), overlap considerably. Groups are of two types: some are effectively bachelor parties that solely contain a mixture of juvenile, adolescent and adult males. Breeding groups consist of a single dominant male, together with females of all ages and younger males that have not yet been forced to depart into a bachelor group. Bachelor groups often contain more individuals. Groups regularly come together and associate during the evening, when they sleep close to rivers; they may also meet and travel together during the day.

During the course of a day they can travel long distances, up and down forest adjacent to the river and even across it. However, they very rarely stray more than 600m (2,000 feet) in from the river, hence their home ranges effectively constitute a series of long, thin strips following waterways. Groups always return to trees at river edges to sleep, the assumption being that this reduces the likelihood of being ambushed by a predator.

In the morning, it is normally the females that take the lead and begin the daily activities: adult males are generally the last individuals to leave the sleep site.

Proboscis Monkeys are also highly vocal, and have a repertoire of various roars, grunts, groans, squeals and honks: when looking for them it is often the case that they are first heard rather than seen – from a distance, groups might be compared to a gaggle of grumbling old men. Some calls demonstrate aggression, others excitement, and some help calm subordinate members of the group.

Apes

Apes are our closest living relatives. While the high-profile species in Africa (Gorillas, Chimpanzees and Bonobos) tend to steal the limelight, it is easy to overlook the fact that the majority of ape species actually live in South-East Asia. There are 13 species in South-East Asia (not counting humans), 11 of which are various types of gibbon, collectively known as the Lesser Apes (family Hylobatidae), and two species of Orang-utan from the Great Apes (family Hominidae).

Unlike all other primates, apes have no tail (some other primates such as the Slow Loris and Indri from Madagascar have very small vestigial tails), and their forelimbs tend to be longer than the hind limbs, as they are predominant in locomotion. Coupled with this, the chest is expanded because of the increased musculature associated with strong forearms.

Gibbons

For a demonstration of sheer exuberance, few animals can compete with a gibbon. To watch one swing extravagantly and effortlessly through the canopy is to witness an animal totally at one with its environment, and seemingly revelling in the fact that it can do something other species cannot. The method of traversing the tree tops they have perfected – suspended beneath branches and swinging arm to arm – is called 'brachiation'. Gibbons epitomize this, and no other primate can move through the canopy with such speed and agility. However, this is not without its risks, and tumbles do occur when branches snap or gaps are misjudged. Indeed, most individuals suffer bone fractures during their lives, and some animals are killed as a result of falls.

Two species with non-overlapping ranges occur on Borneo: the Agile Gibbon (*Hylobates agilis*) is restricted to parts of west and central Kalimantan in the south-west of the island (it also occurs in southern Sumatra and parts of Peninsula Malaysia), while the Bornean or Müller's Gibbon (*Hylobates muelleri*) is

SINGING IN THE RAINFOREST

There are few sounds in nature more evocative than the whooping song of a gibbon; it is a sound that encapsulates so much of the spine-tingling spirit and mystery of Borneo. Yet these songs, performed by both sexes, are highly complex, and their subtleties and nuances are far from fully understood.

The song sequences of males and females are very different in both form and function. Males may perform individually, often beginning well before sunrise, but finishing shortly after dawn. This begins as a series of gentle warblings, but builds with time over 20 or so minutes into a loud, elaborate song. Females, on the other hand, often sing in the mid-morning, and their song is shorter and less varied in its composition of notes, but may be repeated over and over.

It is assumed that the song's primary function is to alert other gibbons to their presence and place in the forest. Lone male solos may be advertisements by individuals seeking a mate, while paired males probably sing to defend their mate from the attentions of other males. Female songs probably relate to her defence of fruiting trees from other females; consequently they sing less frequently when animals are dispersed, but may sing daily if gibbon densities in their area are high. Fights do occur but are rare (because of the high risks), and generally only take place when new individuals move into an area.

At times, males accompany females and create complex duets. While the intricacy of these varies between the different species of gibbon, the degree of synchronization between the sexes during their duet increases with practice, and so the quality of their combined song is directly co-related to the length of time the couple has been together.

found to the north of the Kapuas and east of the Barito rivers; this range encompasses parts of Kalimantan and most of Sawawak, Brunei and Sabah, where there is suitable habitat.

Being almost exclusively arboreal, gibbons are inextricably linked with native forest areas, preferring lowland dipterocarp and lower elevations of hill dipterocarp forest, where they feed mainly on soft fruits. They do not live in large troops like monkeys, but instead form monogamous family units – an adult pair with one or two offspring from previous years – that occupy territories of around two to three hectares. Loud melodic calls, performed by both males and females, are the primary means of territorial defence. Early in the morning adult pairs often perform melancholic duets that help strengthen pair bonds and proclaim their residence in an area of forest.

The Orang-utan

Perhaps more than any other animal, the Orang-utan is synonymous with Borneo. However, Orang-utans are not restricted to the island: one species, the Sumatran Orang-utan, is now confined to the forests at the very northern tip of its eponymous island, while the Bornean Orang-utan (*Pongo pygmaeus*) by comparison is much more widespread on its island home. Nonetheless, the Bornean Orang-utan also finds the boundaries of its habitat shrinking in the face of human development and expansion.

The Orang-utan's appeal is instant and compelling. Hold the inquisitive gaze of an infant, and it is only too apparent how narrow is the 15 million years of evolutionary separation. Our facial expressions are mirror images of one another, and the depth of thought and intelligence behind their emotion-filled eyes is unerringly close to our perception of self. They are also tool-users; for instance, in a torrential downpour they will pluck off a large leaf and hold it above their head as an umbrella – and their resigned 'fed-up and frustrated' look is as instantly identifiable as any of our own expressions while standing at the bus stop in the rain.

While genetic studies have confirmed that the Bonobo or

ABOVE: *At times, male Orang-utans (Pongo pygmaeus) can be very vocal, and calls can carry up to one kilometre (0.62 miles).*

Pygmy Chimpanzee is actually our closest living relative (a staggering 98.4 per cent of our genes are the same), we still share over 96 per cent of our genetic material with Orang-utans. That said, the Orang-utan is quite different in many ways from the Great Apes from Africa.

Chimpanzees and gorillas are largely terrestrial, and move primarily by 'knuckle-walking'; in contrast, the Orang-utan is almost exclusively arboreal (it is in fact the world's largest tree-dwelling animal). Its forearms are 30 per cent longer than its legs, and both the hands and feet are equally adept at gripping (the hands have opposable thumbs, the feet opposable big toes). Orang-utans clamber around the canopy, always maintaining hold of branches with at least two of their limbs, and can suspend themselves upside down from both feet. However, they are unable to jump, and span gaps by forcing a tree to swing back and forth until they can reach adjacent

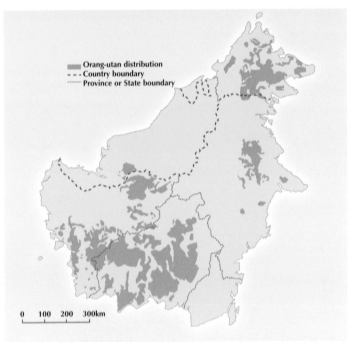

Orang-utan distribution
– – – Country boundary
········ Province or State boundary

0   100   200   300km

ABOVE: *Orang-utans (Pongo pygmaeus) can gorge themselves on fruit, and are happy to spend all day feeding from a fruit-laden tree.*

branches as the gap narrows. Very large males can be too heavy to move across some gaps, and are forced to descend the tree trunk, move across the ground and then ascend the next tree.

Being very large, sleeping high in the canopy is not without its problems. Obviously, many tree-top branches are incapable of supporting their weight alone, and being narrow, it would be rather hazardous simply to try and perch on one to sleep (in the way many monkeys do). The Orang-utan's solution is to build a nest. A new nest is constructed daily, and as evening approaches, an individual will select a suitable spot. This is often in a tree fork with plenty of thin, twiggy, leafy branches around, which the Orang-utan folds inwards and underneath itself, as well as weaving in other branches that it snaps off. The

end result is, in effect, a sleeping platform up to 1m (3.3 feet) across, on which the animal curls up for the night. Being solitary, they always sleep alone, although mothers sleep with their offspring. Young Orang-utans show the first signs of play nest-building behaviour by around four years, although they are generally five to seven before they actually make and use their own nests. By choice, a youngster will continue to sleep with its mother in her nest until she stops this practice; normally this happens only after she has given birth to her next offspring.

Biology and behaviour
In both sexes, the hair is long, straight and reddish-orange in colour. There can be considerable variation between individuals, and coat colour may change with age: juveniles may be fairly bright orange, while some old animals are maroon or very dark, chocolate brown. The face is always bare and is generally dark, with paler areas around the eyes and

mouth, particularly in younger animals, although these darken with age. Males have a throat pouch and cheek pads of fatty tissue that develop into a large facial disc in mature animals.

The Bornean Orang-utan is endemic to the island, where it is found in lowland and medium-elevation rainforest (up to around 1400m/4600 feet), including dipterocarp, riverine and peat-swamp forest. Historical and more recent hunting, and continued deforestation, means their range is restricted to south-west, central and parts of eastern, a few areas in the south-west of Sarawak, areas in eastern and central Sabah and possibly parts of north-west Sabah.

Orang-utans are solitary creatures: as adults they lead socially reclusive lives, foraging alone over very large areas of forest. On average they may travel around 1000m (3,280 feet) in a day, but will move much larger distances in search of food at particular times of fruiting. Adult females with young do not travel alone. Indeed, other than when males and females come

ABOVE: *The diet of Orang-utans* (Pongo pygmaeus) *includes the fruit of many species, particularly those with high sugar quantities.*

together to breed, the only time Orang-utans see each other is when two or more may congregate in a particular large tree laden with ripe fruit. Even under these circumstances, there is often little visible interaction between individuals.

Females breed for the first time between 12 and 15 years of age, and while males may become sexually mature at a similar age, they are certainly not old enough to be dominant, and are therefore unlikely to gain access to receptive females. When reproductively receptive, a female may attract the attentions of more than one male, but she is highly selective. Only dominant males with fully developed cheek flanges and throat pouch are likely to be accepted. These males signify their dominance with what are known as 'long calls' that begin as gravelly, burbling grunts, and build to a roar-like crescendo,

OPPOSITE: *While seeing them at close quarters in rehabilitation centres is memorable, sightings of genuine wild Orang-utans* (Pongo pygmaeus), *like this one in Danum Valley are utterly thrilling.*

RIGHT: *Orang-utans are the most arboreal of the Great Apes, with most individuals spending the majority of their lives in the tree-tops. Large males are sometimes forced to the ground when canopy branches cannot support their considerable weight.*

when the male often shakes nearby branches violently. So loud are these calls that they can be heard up to a kilometre away.

Females give birth to a single offspring every seven to eight years. When travelling, young are carried continuously by their mothers for three to four years, and they continue to sleep together in the mother's nest until she has her next offspring. Offspring do not become independent until at least seven, and often up to ten years. In the wild, a female may live to 40 years, but with such long inter-birth intervals, she will likely only produce four surviving offspring at the most in a lifetime. This is the slowest breeding rate of any primate, and is a major reason why Orang-utan populations recover so slowly.

The Orang-utans' diet is dominated by fruit, for which they have a huge capacity. Being big animals, they have big appetites, and around half the day can be spent feeding. Wild figs are a particular favourite, and if a laden tree is discovered, an individual can remain in it for a day or more, gorging itself. However, a wide variety of other pulpy fruits with a high sugar content are also eaten (over 400 different species have been recorded). When fruit is scarce, leaves, bark, honey, small insects and even birds' eggs may also be consumed.

In Borneo, there are several places where sightings of rehabilitated and released animals are virtually guaranteed: Sepilok Orang-utan Rehabilitation Centre in Sabah, Matang Wildlife Centre and Semenggoh Rehabilitation Centre in Sarawak, Nyaru Menteng, near Palangka Raya and Tanjung Puting National Park in Central Kalimantan.

Seeing truly wild Orang-utans is a more difficult proposition. Because they do not have fixed ranges, and because they move around over large tracts of forest, their whereabouts is very unpredictable, and varies from season to season. However, two locations in Sabah and two in Kalimantan offer a good chance of success, provided you have plenty of time and patience (and luck).

The forest around Borneo Rainforest Lodge in Danum Valley is perhaps the best location in which to view Orang-utans. The undisturbed, towering lowland dipterocarp forest is perfect Orang-utan habitat, and individuals are resident in the vicinity most of the year. If during your stay, you are fortunate enough

to find a fruiting fig or similar tree, there is a good chance an Orang-utan will find it too. And if you are very lucky, Orang-utans are sometimes seen at relatively close quarters in the tree tops from the canopy walkway. But even if you stay for several nights, do not assume a sighting, as there are times when even the lodge guides fail to see one for over a week.

The alternative prime location is the Lower Kinabatangan Wildlife Sanctuary, particularly the forest areas around Sukau where most of the tourist lodges are situated. This mosaic of protected riverine forest blocks is best accessed by boat along the main Kinabatangan river, or along small tributaries such as the Menanggol river. Orang-utans are regularly seen from the water, especially when large trees are in fruit close to the banks. Although accessible by road, it is more rewarding to travel to Sukau by boat from Sandakan. The journey takes around four hours, and during the second half of the trip, the wildlife-watching along the river can be excellent.

Tanjung Puting in Central Kalimantan is difficult to reach, but for the adventurous it offers fantastic opportunities. It is necessary to join a trip into the National Park led specially by members of staff involved with Orang-utan research.

Orang-utan Rehabilitation

It is ironic that, on an island so rich in biodiversity, one of Borneo's major tourist attractions is a facility synonymous with captive and semi-captive animals. Virtually every visitor to

ABOVE: *Orphaned Orang-utans* (Pongo pygmaeus) *require constant care if they are to survive and be successfully rehabilitated.*

Sabah, whether on a beach holiday or wildlife-watching tour, finds time to take in Sepilok Orang-utan Rehabilitation Centre. It is easy to see why: sightings of Orang-utans are almost guaranteed, and encounters often turn into intimate experiences that linger long in the memory.

Established in 1964, Sepilok is the oldest and most accessible of six major rehabilitation centres in Borneo. There are also three in Kalimantan and two in Sarawak. But what exactly do these centres do, and why are they necessary? In a nutshell, they provide a home and safe haven for orphaned and illegally captive Orang-utans, with the intention of returning them firstly to full health, and then back to the wild. Their underlying rationale is a combination of individual animal welfare and species conservation. Most centres also include public education on conservation and research, and assistance to other endangered species.

Orang-utans become orphaned primarily because their forest homes are being destroyed and because adults, including mothers with young, are killed when they stray into palm oil plantations (particularly in Kalimantan). Further, as a consequence of being orphaned by habitat loss, some babies are taken for the illegal pet trade (their mothers are killed and the babies are taken to market, and occasionally, exported).

Orphaned and confiscated animals then by varied means find their way to a rehabilitation centre. The majority are young animals, often in poor health. The ordeals and traumas they have endured means they regularly suffer from stress, depression and malnutrition, and sometimes also diseases contracted from humans (anything from colds to tuberculosis).

After an initial period in quarantine, the tiniest infants require constant attention and are cared for around the clock. Older infants (one to three years) are housed with other youngsters in nurseries, with climbing areas and an environment enriched with real branches and foliage. In the wild, young Orang-utans learn the skills necessary for survival from their mothers; this includes climbing, nest building and foraging techniques. Deprived of this, youngsters need help from their human caretakers to gain confidence when climbing. In the nursery environment, juveniles gain confidence when climbing, build up their muscles and develop relationships with the other Orang-utans.

As they get older, their interaction with humans is reduced, and they are introduced to semi-wild areas with natural forest, where they can further develop the climbing, foraging and nest-building skills that are crucial. Finally, when they are sufficiently strong and healthy, they are 'soft-released' into forest areas, where food to supplement their diet is offered daily at a platform. These free meals are kept basic and constant (usually milk and fruit like bananas, plus vital minerals and vitamins), and are not meant to provide the Orang-utans with all their nutritional needs. This prevents them becoming reliant on handouts, and encourages them to forage for themselves; with time, their dependence on this food diminishes, and they return less frequently.

The way Orang-utans are returned to the wild does vary between the various rehabilitation centres. For instance, at Sepilok and most other centres, individuals are able to integrate gradually into native forest that lies adjacent to the rehabilitation centre (the Kabili Forest Reserve). To date, over 100 Orang-utans have been returned, and some of these animals have now bred with the wild population in the area. Adult animals may also be translocated to other forest areas in Sabah, such as the Lower Kinabatangan or Tabin Wildlife Reserve. Funding for this comes from both the state government in Sabah, and from fees paid by visitors to the centre, with additional money being raised by independent charities such as the Sepilok Orang-utan Appeal UK.

In Kalimantan there are three centres: Nyaru Menteng, near Palangka Raya in Central Kalimantan; Wanariset, near Balikpapan in East Kalimantan; and the Orang-utan Care Centre and Quarantine Facility in Central Kalimantan. At all of these sites, Orang-utans ready for release are taken from the centres and released into protected forests elsewhere, that

A QUESTIONABLE EXPENDITURE?

Opponents of Orang-utan rehabilitation centres claim the money would be better spent exclusively on in situ conservation dealing only with wild Orang-utans. These opponents argue that rehabilitation is sentimental, and diverts attention and funding from the issue of saving wild populations. In reality, there is room and necessity for both.

The preservation of all remaining wild populations is of paramount importance, but the numbers of orphaned animals is huge and cannot be overlooked. If not rehabilitation, then what is the alternative? There is no escaping the fact that rehabilitation is an intensive, expensive procedure that is variable in its success. However, rehabilitated individuals have integrated back into wild populations successfully, and help boost numbers in areas of forest able to support them. Further, rehabilitation centres raise public awareness to a level that would be otherwise unobtainable.

have few or no wild Orang-utans. Newly released animals are then followed and monitored closely by dedicated staff who oversee their transition to independence in the wild.

It is estimated that there are over 700 Orang-utans housed at these three centres alone, 250 of which are in the facility near Tanjung Puting, largely funded by the Orang-utan Foundation. Tanjung Puting National Park is now thought to have around 5,000 wild Orang-utans, so no further releases take place. Instead, animals are now released in Lamandau, a newly gazetted nature reserve created from an expired logging concession to the west of Tanjung Puting itself. To date, over 100 rehabilitated animals have been released in Lamandau, along with a number of adults translocated from other sites.

Nocturnal Primates

While some of Borneo's monkeys and apes are well known and conspicuous, the island is also home to two rather shy and secretive species that are only active after dark. Tracking them down is a challenge, but the resulting encounter is worth it.

The Slow Loris

Large, 'doey' eyes, soft fur and cute features make the Slow Loris (*Nycticebus coucang*) one of Borneo's most endearing creatures (see page 97). They belong to a group known as the Strepsirhine primates (formerly referred to as prosimians, which literally means 'before monkeys') that also includes lemurs, pottos, bushbabies and galagos. As a group, they retain some features similar to those of the earliest primates, and are consequently often erroneously referred to as 'primitive'. This is misleading, as they collectively have a number of highly specialized and evolved features. One fundamental 'primitive' characteristic is shared by them all: they do not have a truly opposable thumb and forefinger (something that monkeys, apes and tarsiers do possess); rather, they are only capable of whole-hand grasping.

As their name implies, Slow Lorises generally take life at a rather sedate pace; their fore and hind limbs are roughly equal in length, and they creep, climb and walk along branches rather than leap between them. However, if alarmed or disturbed, they are capable of a surprising turn of speed. They also have very short vestigial tails; obviously their chosen mode of locomotion does not require the longer counterbalance tail possessed by more active primates. In common with their cousins, the lemurs (from Madagascar), lorises are heavily reliant on their sense of smell, and their relatively long muzzle is testimony to this. The soft pulp of ripe fruits and some insects form the bulk of their diet, and they are even able to eat unpalatable prey such as poisonous millipedes. It is thought that their slow metabolism allows time for the toxins to be neutralized before they are absorbed and have a chance to take effect.

The Tarsier

The second nocturnal primate is the tarsier, which is amongst the most unusual and remarkable of primates. Five species are found variously in the forests of Sumatra, Borneo, Sulawesi and the Philippines, all resembling Lilliputian Hollywood gremlins; however, only one of these, the Western Tarsier (*Tarsius bancanus*), occurs on Borneo. Relative to their body size, they have the biggest eyes of any mammal. Each eye has a diameter of around 16mm (0.6 inches) and weighs 3g (0.1 ounces), which is slightly more than the tarsier's brain!

Weighing in at little more than 100-120g (3-4 ounces), the Western Tarsier is Borneo's smallest primate. Indeed, amongst the world's primates, only the Dwarf Bushbaby (*Galago demidoff*) from Central and West Africa and the mouse lemurs (*Microcebus* spp.) from Madagascar are smaller. However, small size has not prevented them from becoming phenomenal athletes. Powered by long hind limbs, these typical 'vertical clingers and leapers' are capable of jumps in excess of 40 times their own body length, allowing them to ricochet between thin tree trunks and saplings in the forest understorey in pursuit of their prey. Their diet consists solely of animal protein, including insects such as moths, katydids, beetles and cicadas, and occasionally, vertebrates such as frogs and small lizards. They have even been known to catch and kill small birds and small venomous snakes.

Being a nocturnal hunter, it is not surprising that the tarsier's eyes are large; however, their disproportionate size is a clue to their evolutionary history. All other nocturnal primates (for instance, the Slow Loris), have highly reflective eyes, the result of the *tapetum lucidum*, a layer at the back of the eye which maximizes its light-capturing capability. When diurnal primates evolved, this layer became superfluous and disappeared. The tarsiers' ancestors were thus probably diurnal, and they have subsequently become secondarily adapted to life in the dark once again. To make up for the lack of a reflective layer, their eyes have become huge to maximize their light-gathering capacity and efficiency.

They are hard to locate, however, as the red reflected eye-shine typical of other nocturnal primates is absent. While known to occur in many lowland areas in Kalimantan, Sarawak, Brunei and Sabah, they rarely appear to venture into upland areas above 1000m (3300 feet). Sabah's Danum Valley is the best place to look for tarsiers.

In common with many nocturnal primates, both lorises and tarsiers are solitary for much of the time, although individuals may meet where their ranges overlap at various times during the night, and may interact, sometimes grooming one another.

THE PEOPLE OF BORNEO

The diversity of cultures on Borneo is as varied and distinct as the island's fauna and flora: there are known to be well over 150 languages and dialects that are still in use in various parts of the island today. While there is evidence that the earliest human habitation on the island may date back at least 40,000 years, the ancestors of today's indigenous populations probably began to settle around 4,500 years ago. It is thought that these early colonists were Austronesian, and that they perhaps migrated to Borneo from the Philippines, having originally come from China via Taiwan. Initially, these people would have been restricted to the areas immediately around the coast, but once the use of iron and other metals had spread to Borneo, they were better able to exploit the rainforests, and began moving further into the interior.

INDIGENOUS CULTURE AND TRADE

The indigenous peoples of the island of Borneo, collectively called Dayaks in Kalimantan and Sarawak, are a diverse group that practice various forms of shifting cultivation, in which the production of rice is always central.

Collectively, the indigenous agricultural populations of Borneo were referred to by Dutch and British settlers as 'Dayaks', although this is by no means a precise term, as it encompasses a multitude of distinct ethnic groups and peoples. Rice is considered a sacred crop, and is a common thread that connects the many tribes: its cultivation is both religious and economic and is at the centre of Dayak culture. So germane is rice that in some Dayak languages, the word for food translates directly as 'rice'. Traditionally, the Dayaks have used a system of 'slash and burn' shifting cultivation or swidden agriculture to grow rice, and in most instances, this practice persists to this day.

The Dayak ethos maintains that their lives are inextricably linked with their environment, and their vision of prosperity links rivers, land and forests as essential components of the Dayak identity. These beliefs are reflected in their approach to a shifting mosaic of land use that intertwines the forests and cultivation.

Typically, areas around Dayak villages incorporate patches of natural forest, cultivated forest, cultivated fields, fallow land and permanent gardens. The composition of these mosaics varies according to the area concerned, whether mountain, wetland or river valley. Only permanent rice paddies constitute completely non-forested areas.

While there is no doubt that these traditional shifting practices do have a negative impact on the rainforest, the impact is in most areas localized and limited when weighed against the ravages of industrial forest conversion to plantations. Studies in the 1950s suggested that only 5 per cent of clearing for shifting cultivation takes place in primary forest,

while the vast majority is on fallow land. Compare this to the tens of thousands of hectares of forest that are felled or burned each year by immigrant farmers from other parts of Indonesia, by plantation developers and through El Nino fires, and the minimal impact of indigenous farmers is all too apparent. The agricultural practices of the Dayaks have largely been in harmony with the broader landscape for hundreds of years, and it is only since the large-scale exploitation of industrial logging and conversion to monoculture cash crops that deforestation and soil erosion have become such pressing – and depressing – issues.

Dayak Groups

The Dayaks as a whole can be sub-divided into numerous groups that correlate to differences in the way their societies are governed, from those that are egalitarian to others that are hierarchical. The Keyan-Kenyah are the most dominant group in central Borneo, while the Kelabit-Lun Bawang group are found where Sarawak, Sabah, Brunei and Kalimantan all border one another. The Iban are the largest group, and were previously called Sea-Dayaks because of their association with coastal regions, particularly in West Kalimantan. The Bidayuh have also been called Land-Dayaks, and like the Iban, they live in egalitarian societies. The Barito cover much of the southern regions of the island, and the Dusun-Kadazan-Murut group live largely in the north-eastern part of Borneo.

The Penan

The nomadic Penan are a group that warrant particular mention, as they have not turned to agriculture and shifting cultivation; rather, they have remained as a remnant population of

PREVIOUS PAGE: *Dursun tribal communities inhabit the north eastern part of Borneo. They place high value on many ancient artefacts, including brass gongs that are used during traditional ceremonies.*

OPPOSITE: *Murut tribes staunchly clung to traditional ways of life, including living in longhouses, until relatively recently. The plumes of various forest birds frequently adorned head dresses.*

ABOVE: *Originally from the Kapuas River and the coastal regions of Kalimantan, the Iban slowly spread into Sarawak.*

RIGHT: *The institution of pejalai (bejalah), where young men travel to gain wealth and experience, is an important part of Iban culture. Numerous tattoos testify to the extent of a man's travels.*

traditionally nomadic hunter-gatherers, and have managed to maintain this lifestyle despite the influence and encroachment of modern living.

Today, the Penan are few in number; in Sarawak, for instance, there may be no more than 500 who remain truly nomadic. As has always been the case, traditional Penan depend heavily on a healthy forest ecosystem for their daily subsistence, which means that they invariably live in enclaves of primary forest surrounded by farming Dayak communities, although there is trade between the groups.

Penan subsistence is dependent on sago palms, from which they collect high energy flour, and their movements around the forest are determined by the availability of this food-stuff. In addition, a large variety of fruits are eaten; the Penan also hunt for Bearded Pigs using spears, and for primates as well, using blow pipes.

Wildlife Trade and Hunting

The trade in animal parts and products is an ancient one. An established trading route between the north-west coast of Borneo (now Sarawak and Brunei) and China dates back to at least 700 AD, and possibly before. This not only involved commodities such as timber, spices, fruits and precious metals, but also animals, dead and alive, part and whole. The most highly valued were the horns of the Asian Two-horned Rhinoceros, 'hornbill ivory', and edible birds' nests. There was also an important trade in the ornate feathers of many species that were used for jewellery. Fortunately the trade in 'hornbill ivory' – the intricately carved casques of Helmeted Hornbills – and feathers has now largely ceased, although tribes in the interior of Borneo still hunt Argus Pheasants, Peacock Pheasants and many of the large hornbills for their feathers, to decorate ceremonial costumes.

However, the trade in rhino horn and edible birds' nests is still very much alive, and is only a small part of a vast network of wildlife trade that is historically and culturally entrenched in South-East Asia. For centuries this trade had continued largely at a level of subsistence, supplying local demands at levels that were sustainable in the long term. As such, the trade contributed to sustaining community livelihoods, maintaining cultural values and generating revenue, both locally and nationally.

But over the last 40 years, this subsistence tick-over has grown to a rampant commercial trade, fuelled largely by economic growth in the region, leading to increases in demand and purchasing power in the marketplace. As of 2005, the smuggling of protected species in Indonesia alone is a business estimated to be worth around US$1.4 billion per year. The considerable impact on species populations in Borneo has profound implications for conservation.

Throughout South-East Asia there is a complex chain of supply, partnered with diversifying consumer demand that makes conservation and management of wild species challenging. Consumption patterns alter with market force changes, but the consistent demand for some species favoured as traditional medicines, in the exotic pet industry, as

OPPOSITE: *Large snakes like the Reticulated Python (Python reticulatus) are widely hunted for their meat and beautiful skins.*

BELOW: *Centuries of hunting for its horn to supply traditional medecinal markets have resulted in the Sumatran Rhinoceros being the most endangered large animal on Borneo.*

ornaments, in private zoo collections and as 'tonic' food items is now so high that many species face terminal declines in their populations, and ultimately, extinction.

Once a species reaches market, it is often impossible to determine from exactly where it might have come, but there is no doubt a significant quantity of the species that appear in the markets of Indonesia, Thailand, Vietnam, China, and even further afield, originate in Borneo. These include high-profile species such as Orang-utans (that can fetch as much as US$25,000) and gibbons for the prestige pet trade, together with pythons and other reptiles. Estimates from TRAFFIC South-East Asia (TRAFFIC is a joint programme run by the World Wide Fund for Nature (WWF) and the International Union for the Conservation of Nature (IUCN), investigating the trade in fauna and flora worldwide) suggest that several hundred young Orang-utans may be illegally exported from Kalimantan each year for sale in markets in Java, Bali and elsewhere.

Traditional medicinal practices assign miraculous properties to powders and potions made from all manner of body parts from a huge diversity of species, perhaps the most high profile being tiger bone and other body parts. While this particular example is not relevant to Borneo (because tigers are absent),

the trade does severely affect numerous other species on the island. For instance, powdered rhino horn is used as a medicine to combat fever and pain; the bile and gall bladders of Sun Bears are thought to cure internal injuries; the wrist glands of Slow Loris and the scent glands of several civets are prized for various uses, and Pangolin scales are believed to have magical healing powers, and are thought to cure a broad spectrum of ailments including allergies, skin conditions and even sexually transmitted diseases!

Species collected as fashionable or 'tonic' foods not only include edible birds' nests, but also freshwater turtles, marine turtles and their eggs, some other reptiles, particularly large snakes like pythons, and venomous species such as cobras and even Pangolins. Further, many species are traded for their skins: these include the pelts of wild cats such as Clouded Leopards and Marbled Cats, and also the skins of Reticulated Pythons, crocodiles and even Pangolins (again), because they produce distinctively patterned leather for shoes, handbags and other accessories, which appeals to consumers with an inappropriate taste for the exotic.

The trade is not restricted to animal species. In Peninsular Malaysia, Thailand and Sumatra, dried *Rafflesia* buds and flowers have long been used in traditional

OPPOSITE: *The nests of cave swiftlets are big business, so much so that strict regulations are enforced in an attempt to make the harvesting sustainable. In some areas, 'artificial caves' have been constructed to encourage nesting and boost falling swiftlet numbers.*

BELOW: *The instant appeal and cuteness of infant Orang-utans* (Pongo pygmaeus) *have made them highly prized 'prestige' pets, fuelling an expanding illegal trade.*

medicines, particularly during childbirth and to restore fatigue. Historically, there are no apparent uses for the flower in Sabah; instead, it has been regarded as a 'flower of the spirits', and taboo in local cultures. However, in the modern age of communication, information from elsewhere has changed perceptions, and locals are now beginning to use *Rafflesia* blooms and buds; moreover, they can sometimes be seen for sale on roadside stalls in the interior.

Pitcher plants, and in particular, orchids, are also attracting the attention of horticulturalists and hobbyists the world over. Species from Borneo are beautiful and rare, and are regarded as highly desirable, so much so that fanatics are willing to pay considerable sums (hundreds to thousands of dollars), which has created an illicit clandestine trade. In general, the rarer a species becomes, the greater the scarcity component of its price and pressure to obtain the few remaining individuals increases.

The trade in fauna and flora is controlled by the Convention on International Trade in Endangered Species of Wild Fauna and Flora. More conveniently known as CITES, it has been the largest and, some would say, most effective international wildlife conservation agreement. Nonetheless, many member states have demonstrated limited powers to enforce laws effectively, and the high demand and vast sums of money involved in some instances drive the markets for further exploitation. TRAFFIC is working tirelessly to monitor all forms of illegal trade, expose as many of the ringleaders as possible, and ultimately bring those responsible to justice. However, effective law enforcement will only ever provide a rearguard action in the fight against such trade. In the long term, the only effective solution will be to curtail demand for the commodities in the marketplace: without a market, there is no trade to supply. However, this will only happen after major alterations in cultural thinking and the abandonment of ingrained traditional practices.

The three Bornean countries, as members of ASEAN (the Association of South East-Asian Nations), have now agreed to a regional action plan to ensure sustainability of wildlife trade. This will provide a framework to stem illegal trade and enhance the management of legal trade consistent with the 'Heart of Borneo – Three Countries, One Conservation Vision' initiative.

THE HEART OF BORNEO

Rainforests are the lungs of the globe. Although they cover only a fraction of the world's surface, they produce a disproportionately high amount of the planet's oxygen. This not only helps maintain the air that we and the majority of other species breathe, it also helps maintain a healthy, balanced atmosphere that in turn controls and buffers the world's climate. Without rainforests, this delicate balance is terminally disrupted: without rainforests we could not breathe: without rainforests we die. Yet conserving the world's tropical rainforests is not an easy proposition, as there are many conflicting factors. One of the most pressing difficulties is that the major rainforest areas correspond to many of the world's poorest countries, the governments of which are preoccupied with the short-term needs of their people rather than long-term planning for planetary health. It desperately needs to be understood that these two needs are inextricably linked: people can only prosper on a vibrant planet, the life-support systems of which are in full working order.

THE HEART OF BORNEO PROJECT

Life is not evenly spread around planet Earth. Tropical rainforest provides a perfect combination of warmth and water, and no other environment is as species-rich and diverse. To maintain this diversity and the rainforest life-support systems, large areas of continuous forest must be preserved.

When Borneo was pristine, it was cloaked in an endless blanket of forest. Human expansion, exploitation and development have shredded them into lots of small pieces. If the forests become too fragmented, their ability to function efficiently is compromised. Half a rainforest does not contain half the number of original species. It contains far fewer.

It has become apparent that the current network of protected areas (comprised of parks and protection forests) on Borneo are too scattered to effectively protect all species if the intervening forests are converted to non-forest use. The borders of these areas continue to erode due to deforestation, compromised by illegal hunting and trade of endangered species, and undermined by out-of-control forest fires. The full-scale biodiversity of these areas will not be maintained if they become a fragmented patchwork. At current rates of depletion some sources have estimated that, by 2010, all the lowland forest of Kalimantan will be gone, and by 2020 there will be no undisturbed habitat left outside protected areas in the vast upland wildernesses of Borneo.

There is only one place in South-East Asia where rainforest remains on a large enough scale to guarantee permanent viability: Borneo. And it is not quite too late, because the island's interior still harbors unspoiled areas, where biodiversity flourishes. There are rugged hills, cloaked in magnificent virgin forests. Here, the cries of the gibbons still carry through the early morning mist, squadrons of noisy hornbills fly overhead, from understorey to canopy the forest teems with insects, and the forests themselves retain their intact architectural splendour. Major rivers are born as tumbling mountain streams (most of the island's major rivers originate in the region) that broaden and mature as they flow down into the lowlands, where they supply the island's freshwater ecosystems, as well as forming the waterways vital for transport to indigenous peoples. This core area straddles the trans-boundary highlands of Indonesia (Kalimantan) and Malaysia (Sarawak and Sabah), and reaches out through the foothills into adjacent lowlands that encompass parts of

PREVIOUS PAGE: *A thick blanket of mist cloaks pristine lowland forest as the sun's first morning rays catch the canopy.*

LEFT: *Forest fires have ravaged many parts of the island in recent years, particularly in areas of Kalimantan.*

OPPOSITE: *Flourishing populations of large birds, like this Oriental Pied Hornbill (Anthracoceros albirostris), are good indicators of environmental well-being and healthy forest areas.*

Kalimantan, Sarawak, Sabah and Brunei. The World Wide Fund for Nature (WWF) calls this area the 'Heart of Borneo'.

WWF is working with Borneo's three governments under the banner 'Three Countries, One Conservation Vision', to conserve what is one of the last great wilderness areas: the last bastion of South-East Asian rainforest protected on a large enough scale to be permanently viable. The Heart of Borneo covers roughly 220,000 square km (85,000 square miles) – about the size of the United Kingdom) – and its preservation through a network of protected areas and sustainably managed productive forests will ensure the survival of Borneo's unique biodiversity. The total proposed area is approximately 25 per cent of the island's landmass, around 60 per cent of which is in Indonesia, nearly 40 per cent in Malaysia and 1 per cent in Brunei. It is hoped that in 2006, the governments of the three nations that administer Borneo will issue a declaration creating one of the world's largest and richest conservation areas, the extent of which will encompass the area ranging from Buki Baka-Bukit Raya National Park in Central/West Kalimantan to Batang Ai National Park and Lanjak Entimau Wildlife Sanctuary in Sarawak, to Ulu Temburong National Park in Brunei, and on to Crocker Range National Park in north-west Sabah, and east as far as Danum Valley and the Lower Kinabatangan Wildlife Sanctuary.

The biological significance of this core area cannot be overstated. In the past decade (1994-2004) it has seen the discovery of over 360 new species, including 260 insects, 50 plants, 30 freshwater fish, eight frogs, six lizards, five crabs and two snakes. However, in a region that is rugged, remote and still largely unexplored, these represent only a fraction of the

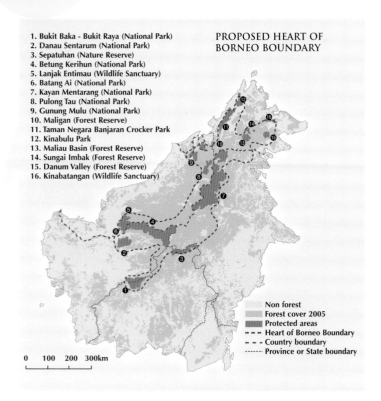

PROPOSED HEART OF
BORNEO BOUNDARY

1. Bukit Baka - Bukit Raya (National Park)
2. Danau Sentarum (National Park)
3. Sepatuhan (Nature Reserve)
4. Betung Kerihun (National Park)
5. Lanjak Entimau (Wildlife Sanctuary)
6. Batang Ai (National Park)
7. Kayan Mentarang (National Park)
8. Pulong Tau (National Park)
9. Gunung Mulu (National Park)
10. Maligan (Forest Reserve)
11. Taman Negara Banjaran Crocker Park
12. Kinabulu Park
13. Maliau Basin (Forest Reserve)
14. Sungai Imbak (Forest Reserve)
15. Danum Valley (Forest Reserve)
16. Kinabatangan (Wildlife Sanctuary)

Non forest
Forest cover 2005
Protected areas
- - - Heart of Borneo Boundary
- - Country boundary
------ Province or State boundary

0   100   200   300km

biological riches from the area, and many more potentially await discovery. The Heart of Borneo aims to maintain this core in very large blocks of inter-connected forest, without which hundreds, or even thousands, of species may become extinct. Its preservation will ensure the integrity of watersheds and, through sustainable management of forest areas, food security and cultural survival for the indigenous peoples of Borneo. This will, in turn, help to alleviate poverty. In the long term, it will help save the island from the ultimate threat of deforestation and increased impacts from droughts and fires.

The phenomenal diversity of species that inhabit the Heart of Borneo shares the landscape with a relatively low density of humans. In themselves, these people are not the greatest threat to the health of the ecosystem: the greatest threat to the Heart of Borneo's forest and wildlife is posed by the commercial logging and large-scale land-clearing initiatives of international corporations. The primary concerns include timber, rubber and wood-pulp operations, and palm-oil plantations on a vast scale, whose product is used in a variety of foodstuffs, cosmetics and fuels largely to supply demand in populous countries such as China and India, and the affluent West.

OPPOSITE: *Occasionally Orang-utans stray into palm oil plantations to feed, where they are persecuted by irate plantation staff.*

ABOVE: *If conservation, development and sustainability are to be successfully achieved, then a balance must be reached between palm-oil plantations like this one and forest preservation.*

A case in point is the Kinabatangan to Sebuku Sembakung corridor, which is an integral part of the Heart of Borneo concept in the north-east of the island. Linking several protected areas and forest reserves, including the Lower Kinabatangan Wildlife Sanctuary, Danum Valley, Maliau Basin and Deramakot Forest in Sabah, as well as the proposed Sebuku Sembakung National Park in Kalimantan, the area covers 2.5 million hectares (6.1 million acres) of rainforest. These hectares are the strongholds of several endangered species such as the Bornean Pygmy Elephant, Sumatran Rhino, Orang-utan, Proboscis Monkey and Clouded Leopard. The WWF and its partners say that this vital area should be managed as one unit, with compliance, participation and approval from all stakeholders, from the local village to the ministerial level in Malaysia and Indonesia.

The ever-increasing demand for vegetable oil is a major threat to this region, and has already been responsible for considerable forest fragmentation. A scheme proposed in 2005, to be funded by China, aims to create the world's largest palm-oil plantation in Kalimantan, near the borders with Sarawak and Sabah. This would involve the conversion of 1.8 million hectares (4.5 million acres) of forest in a mostly mountainous region that is an integral part of the Heart of Borneo. WWF has been quick to stress that the proposal is badly conceived, not least because the proposed areas comprise mainly steep slopes with infertile soils at higher altitudes, and are totally unsuitable for the cultivation of oil palms. If this project is given the 'green light' it will not only have a devastating effect on the biodiversity of the region, but will also have a long-lasting impact on the local people who depend on the area and its freshwater resources. Instead, our vision should be to accept that a lot more oil-palm plantations are needed to supply world demand for vegetable oils, to identify where these will be, and for all stakeholders (relevant governments, producers, buyers, consumers and conservationists) to work together for a solution. If some of the plantations are to be in Borneo, they should be mainly in Kalimantan, where there are many rural people heading for poverty as timber runs out and in need of alternative regular income sources, and where there are vast areas of degraded forests on degraded lands.

In other words, this is no time to shirk in the face of adversity, nor to digress into local short-term issues when a global, long-term approach is needed. The first important steps have been taken to convert this unique opportunity into a workable reality, thus conserving one quarter of the world's third largest island. As the vision for the Heart of Borneo initiative states: 'It is now or never.'

THE SUMMIT OF BORNEO: MOUNT KINABALU

On an island that is predominantly covered in lowland forest – only 6 per cent of the whole island is above 1000m (3,300 feet) elevation – it is not surprising that those upland areas that do exist are especially significant. Effectively, they have become high-altitude islands surrounded by a sea of lowland forest. Such isolation has created conditions that have led to the evolution of communities bristling with unusual and locally endemic species.

The precursors of these species are derived from stock that originated from both the Asian and Australasian continental mainlands (when Borneo was part of the Greater Sunda landmass). Thus, these isolated montane areas have become melting pots of diversity, the likes of which are not seen anywhere else on the island of Borneo, and which rival any similar montane habitats on earth.

THE MOUNTAIN: MYTHS AND REALITY

Mount Kinabalu rises like a citadel from the lowlands of northern Borneo. Its summit is 4095m (13,436 feet) above sea level (the highest point between the Himalayas and New Guinea), and it provides the most extreme and spectacular example of this montane isolation effect.

Kinabalu is a mountain that has captured the imagination for centuries: its effect and appeal are instant. In a modern world of shrinking boundaries and perspectives, the mountain still encapsulates all that is mystical and untamed. Its power is enhanced by its isolation.

It is not surrounded by other high peaks that would dilute its splendour; instead it rises with menacing darkness, straight out of verdant green, tropical forest to a multi-peaked summit of stark, bare rock.

The mountain is a huge dome of granite that was forced through the earth's crust as molten rock. These colossal forces caused rippling and folding of the surrounding sedimentary rocks, which formed the neighbouring mountain ranges of Trus Madi and Crocker to the south. This happened in the recent geological past, perhaps only 10 to 15 million years ago, and Kinabalu is still rising by about 5mm (¼ inch) per year. Since its birth, the mountain has been moulded further by glaciers during various ice ages; these flowed from the summit and scoured the great ravines and gullies that are such a feature of the mountain today. Only the very highest peaks stood above the ice, and were eroded into jagged forms. The last ice cap retreated about 8,000 years ago.

PREVIOUS PAGE: *The view from the roof of Borneo: sunrise on the summit of Mount Kinabalu.*

OPPOSITE: *On the upper slopes of the mountain, constant cloud and frequent high rainfall maintains numerous crystal-clear mountain streams, habitats for the tadpoles of mountain frogs.*

BELOW: *A spectacular sunrise over Mount Kinabalu, as viewed from the park headquarters.*

It is not surprising that a mountain with the presence of Kinabalu should feature strongly in local belief and folklore. The indigenous peoples living within sight of the peak, and especially on its slopes, all respect the mountain as a resting place of their dead. They have long been happy to explore its lower slopes, but historically the upper 1000m (3300 feet) were left untouched for the spirits. Fables are also interwoven into the fabric of local beliefs; one tells of dragons guarding treasure near the summit. The exposed quartz crystals and many waterfalls on the granite outcrops often catch the sun and, tantalizingly, glisten like jewels. This may have spawned the many legends accounting tales of diamonds and pearls.

The first person accredited with climbing Kinabalu was Hugh Low (later Sir Hugh); he took nine days to reach the summit plateau in 1851, and travelled with an entourage of 42 people. Coming from a family of horticulturalists, Low was primarily interested in botany, and so taken was he by the wealth and diversity of plants that he found during his first ascent that he climbed the mountain twice more in April and July, 1858. Not only are the mountain's summit, Low's Peak, and the notorious Low's Gully, on the northern side of the mountain, named after him, but a number of plant species are too, including perhaps the most unusually shaped of all pitcher plants, Low's Pitcher Plant (*Nepenthes lowii*).

ABOVE: *The majestic Mount Kinabalu looks both restful and imposing when bathed in late evening light.*

However, Low did not actually reach the summit that bears his name – he only reached the summit plateau – and it was the British zoologist John Whitehead who finally conquered the mountain in 1888, after spending nearly two years collecting specimens on its slopes. At the time, his were the most thorough documentations of the fauna there had ever been, and these documentations provided the basis for much of the research that has taken place subsequently. Several species have been named after him, most notably three of the mountain's endemic birds: Whitehead's Trogon (*Harpactes whiteheadi*), Whitehead's Broadbill (*Calyptomena whiteheadi*) and Whitehead's Spiderhunter (*Arachnothera juliae*).

Today, climbing the mountain is a much easier proposition than it was in those days, and the climb is generally achieved by most who attempt it in two days. On most days, the number of climbers who reach the summit approach 50 to 100: over 30,000 now climb the mountain annually. But Kinabalu Park has so much more to offer, and those who ascend the mountain are only a fraction of the overall number of people (in excess of 230,000 per annum) who enjoy its scenic and biological riches.

Biological Diversity

Kinabalu park covers an area of approximately 750 square km (290 square miles), and the botanical diversity it harbors is remarkable: perhaps as many as 6,000 plant species occur on the mountain (excluding mosses and liverworts). These include more than 1,000 species of orchid (30 per cent of all species on Borneo), over 600 species of fern (more than the entire Continent of Africa), including 50 or so that are endemic, and more than one third of all the islands' pitcher plants (genus *Nepenthes*). To put this into further context, Kinabalu's botanical diversity represents 10 per cent of all plant species recorded in the biogeographical region of Malesia (collectively, this is the Malay Peninsula, Sumatra, Java, Borneo, the Philippines, Sulawesi and New Guinea).

Nor are such diversity superlatives restricted to the botanical world. Take, for examples, the butterflies and moths (order Lepidoptera): over 600 species of butterfly, representing 60 per cent of Borneo's total number, are found on Kinabalu, together with as many as 1,000 out of 10,000 moth species. Further, over 320 species of bird have been seen on the mountain.

The many rivers that originate on the mountain support over 40 species of fish, though virtually none of them are found above 1500m (5,000 feet) in elevation. At this extreme, in the well oxygenated, tumbling waters lives the sucker fish (genus *Gastromyzon*) that has adapted its pectoral fins into a 'sucker' that allows it to cling to rocks in the fast-flowing water while it grazes their surface for algae.

Approximately 78 species of amphibian and 112 species of reptile are known from Mount Kinabalu and its immediate surrounding area, although these figures are sure to rise as new species are still being discovered. The majority are found at lower elevations as the cooler temperatures of higher altitudes do not suit them. Nonetheless, there are species within the montane forests that have become specialized.

There also seems to be a trend towards gigantism on the mountain. While the lower forests boast, for

TOP: *Numerous montane species have their strongholds on Mount Kinabalu; amongst these is the Grey-chinned or Mountain Minivet* (Pericrocotus solaris).

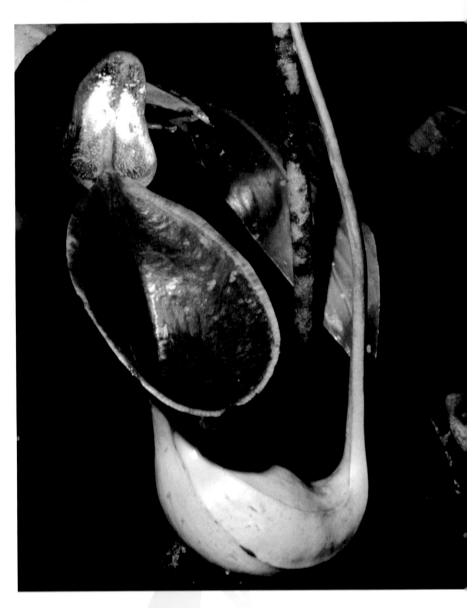

BOTTOM: Low's Pitcher Plant (Nepenthes lowii) *is perhaps the most bizarre of the numerous pitcher plant species that grow on Mount Kinabalu.*

ABOVE: *The Indigo Flycatcher* (Eumyias indigo) *is a common bird around medium elevations on the mountain.*

TOP RIGHT: *The Emerald Flower Beetle* (Pseudochalcothea spathifera) *is the only known species of flower-chafer in the park that is attracted to lights.*

BOTTOM RIGHT: *Given its enormous size, it is comforting that the Kinabalu Giant Leech* (Mimobdella buettikoferi) *preys only on large earthworms.*

instance, the world's largest butterflies and moths, the upper slopes are home to some equally remarkable inhabitants. The Kinabalu Giant Leech reaches lengths of 300mm (12 inches), and preys exclusively on the Kinabalu Giant Earthworm, which can be up to 700mm (28 inches) long!

The full extent of the park's riches are perhaps best appreciated by a gradual ascent, stopping frequently to take in each of the major forest types and the subtle changes that occur with increasing altitude. Diversity of species is greatest on the lower slopes that are covered in lowland rainforest, whereas the greatest numbers of endemic species are found high on the mountain: the more isolated they are, the more specialized and unique they have become.

Changes with Elevation

Most lowland dipterocarp forest from the southern slopes of the mountain has now been removed. Nonetheless, around 35 per cent of the park is covered in this forest type, mainly in the remote north and east. Species richness at these lower elevations is much the same as in similar forests elsewhere on the island. The park's primates are largely restricted to this area, and include Orang-utans, Bornean Gibbons, Grey-leaf and Red-leaf Monkeys, Western Tarsier and Slow Loris.

Above 1000m (3,300 feet) in elevation dramatic changes begin to occur as the average temperature drops and rainfall patterns change. Montane forests derive much of their moisture directly from permanent mists and cloud that envelop higher elevations much of the time. At such moderate altitudes –

between 1200m (3,950 feet) and 1700m (5,580 feet) – this constant cloak of moisture suits many species of oak, chestnut and myrtle. The cooler temperatures means that the decomposition of leaves in the forest happens much more slowly, and consequently peat begins to form.

The forests in the vicinity of the park headquarters at around 1550m (5,086 feet) up to the Timpohon Gate at approximately 1850m (6,070 feet) are typical of lower-elevation montane forest. The many well-maintained trails through this area offer ample opportunity to explore. Open areas and forest edges are often productive places to look for birds, and groups of effusive Chestnut-capped Laughing Thrushes and ebullient Bornean Treepies are common. After dark, several species of stick insect can often be found on foliage next to paths; around one third of Borneo's 300 or so species of phasmid have been found in the park. For those willing to look closely, the beautiful endemic Kinabalu Forest Gecko is also often seen on trails around the park headquarters.

Perhaps the best place to begin the exploration of the area and see a selection of Kinabalu's spectacular flora is in the Mountain Garden near the park's headquarters. Here, amongst a beautiful area of rainforest, examples of some of the unusual species from various parts of the park, including higher altitudes, are grown and displayed in a natural 'showcase'. There is an easy-to-walk series of paths, and many of the species are clearly labelled. Flowering shrubs in and around the garden attract sunbirds, flowerpeckers and flycatchers, while the stream running through the forest is a good place to look for various species of frogs.

With further increases in altitude, species composition changes. On the summit trail above the Timpohon Gate, trees continue to get shorter, and their leaves, smaller, to reduce desiccation, and gradually the forest transforms to upper montane forest at altitudes above 2200m (7,200 feet). Birds such as the Mountain Blackeye, Bornean Stubtail and the skulking Mountain Wren-Warbler are readily seen, as are mammals such as the Mountain Tree Shrew and Mountain Ground Squirrel that often scavenge titbits from picnics left by climbers.

Swirling mists blanket the forest for much of the time above 2200m (7,200 feet), particularly from mid-morning onwards as the clouds build after an often clear night. This is referred to as cloud forest, and the perpetual drenching it receives leads to luxuriant growth in mosses, liverworts and lichens. In the nutrient-poor soils, rhododendrons; many orchids, both epiphytic and terrestrial; and the majority of pitcher plants flourish: between 2000m (6,560 feet) and 3300m (10,830 feet) pitcher plants reach their greatest diversity and abundance, with species such as

BELOW: *The Kinabalu Forest Gecko (*Cyrodactylus baluensis*) is commonly seen on night walks in forests close to the park's headquarters.*

RHODODENDRONS OF BORNEO

The acidic soils and cool, moist conditions that predominate on the middle and higher slopes of Mount Kinabalu ideally suit the requirements of plants belonging to the family *Ericaceae*. In fact, on

Borneo members of this family are rarely seen at lower elevations, but they are common on most mountains. As a family, the *Ericaceae* is well-known, as many popular temperate and sub-tropical garden plants belong to it, most notably perhaps members of the genus *Rhododendron*. The largest genus in the *Ericaceae* family, *Rhododendron* contains over 900 species worldwide, some 300 of which occur in South-East Asia. Borneo is known to harbour about 50 species, and around half of these occur on Mount Kinabalu, a proportion of which are endemic. All of the species on Kinabalu belong to the sub-group *Vireya*, which have characteristic long-tailed seeds. During a climb to the summit, between six and fifteen species may be seen in flower, depending on the time of year.

Exposed ridge tops are favoured locations of species like *R. gracile*, which has large, pale yellow flowers, while *R. borneensis* has tiny red tubular flowers that grow low down. In contrast, stream-sides are the preferred habitat of the epiphytic species *R. crassifolium*, which produces a cluster of bell-shaped, pinky-orange coloured flowers.

Nepenthes tentaculata, N. villosa, N. lowii, N. rajah, N. edwardsiana and *N. kinabaluensis* being found at various localities on the mountain.

Above 3300m (10,830 feet), trees become very gnarled and stunted, and are reduced to shrubs. This is the sub-alpine zone, and is dominated by small conifers and heath rhododendrons. In open areas where water collects, soggy, grassy meadows grow with stands of buttercups and gentians. Stunted trees continue to cling on wherever there is sufficient soil, but in more exposed areas, the soil depth is insufficient for their roots. In the crevices, some mountain orchids cling to life. Biting winds and regular torrential rain stops the majority of plants surviving above 3700m (12,150 feet). Only in the sheltered areas do some dwarf bonsai-like shrubs add a splash of life and colour to the otherwise bare rock.

The Final Push

After a night at the rest house at Panar Laban at 3270m (10,730 feet), the trek to the top of the mountain begins in the early hours of the morning, well before dawn. Between Panar Laban and Sayat-Sayat the last remnants of vegetation eke out an

OPPOSITE TOP: *While not the highest points on the mountain, the peculiar 'Donkey's Ears' are instantly recognizable and constantly visible during a mountain ascent.*

OPPOSITE BOTTOM: *Above 3500m (11,480 feet), trees have all but disappeared, and cushion mosses and similarly hardy species cling to the wind-swept rocks.*

existence in the harsh environment. Along cracks where small quantities of soil form and collect, cushions of moss grow, with stands of hardy sedges and grasses; there are even tiny orchids. On the plateau the granite is bare and bleak and stretches through piles of boulders, towards the summit pyramid of Low's Peak (4095m/13,450 feet). There are other peaks, too, that rise from the rock to create an imposing landscape: the oddly shaped 'Donkey's Ears', the Ugly Sisters (4086m/13,406 feet) and St. John's Peak (4090m/13,420 feet).

The final scramble to the top is fulfilling and breath-taking. If one's timing is good, the peak is reached at dawn, just as the sun lifts over the horizon and casts golden beams of light across the cloud-covered lowland way below. Sunrise on the summit of Borneo is a sight never to be forgotten.

The Mountain: Myths and Reality • 157

ECOTOURISM AND CONSERVATION

Balancing the needs and requirements of conservation and development is a very difficult and emotive issue: natural resource preservation on the one hand, natural resource utilization on the other. The problems become more acute in tropical environments, as they are disproportionately rich 'sinks' for biodiversity, and contain the majority of the world's biological wealth, while at the same time being home to a significant proportion of the planet's human population, the majority of which are very poor. How can their aspirations for a better quality of life be balanced with the need to maintain an intact environment, when it is so often the case that exploitation of that environment is seen as the ticket to that better life? Large-scale conservation initiatives now have local people and communities at their core, and concentrate on finding ways to utilize the environment while maintaining sustainability and long-term economic benefits. Ecotourism is an important mechanism for the existence and health of natural areas and wildlife to be translated into an economic return.

DEVELOPMENT AND THE HEART OF BORNEO

The Western world has largely destroyed its own riches, and the supply of its markets, along with those of Japan, China and India, drives much of the exploitation in the tropics. It is the responsibility of these countries to address this issue, and to facilitate an improvement in the quality of life for those peoples living in the tropical regions that have been plundered.

In the past, the human populations living adjacent to forest areas in the tropics have been regarded as the first line of attack. Their exclusion was seen as the answer: creating a park or reserve and leaving it solely as a preserve for wildlife. However, attempts to exclude local people from these areas and prevent exploitation have proved futile and disastrous in the long term. When people's very survival is entwined with harvesting natural resources, whether animal, vegetable or mineral, even the most draconian legislation tends to be flouted. Consequently, the conservation community at large has realized the need for a change of approach. The issue needs to be addressed from the opposite perspective, and they must *involve* the local people.

Over the past two decades there has been a major shift by global conservation organizations such as the World Wide Fund for Nature (WWF). In addition to working with specific high-profile endangered species such as pandas, tigers, elephants or orang-utans, the organization now places additional emphasis on dealing with the problems of local communities and their needs, as it has become apparent that without a human context, there can be no effective nature conservation.

In essence, the principles are simple. Conservation needs to be linked to improving the standards of living for local people, while at the same time reducing the pressures placed on their environment. However, if these initiatives are to succeed, they must above all else give the local people both a say and a personal stake in the project. By becoming aware that their very existence is inextricably linked to the quality and integrity of their environment, local people have the strongest possible incentive to help ensure that its conservation is a success. No longer are they considered the first line of attack, but rather the last line of defence.

These ideas are now pertinent to the conservation efforts in tropical countries around the globe, and are at the core of the WWF's 'Heart of Borneo' concept. Of course, in this instance the challenges are compounded, as the policies of three federal governments (Indonesia, Malaysia and Brunei) have to be reconciled into one coherent framework for trans-boundary conservation that will facilitate the maintenance of the Heart of Borneo in its broadest sense. The jigsaw is both dynamic and complex, involving not only local people, conservationists and governments, but also those with interests in forestry and logging, water resources, palm oil production, animal exploitation and tourism.

Ecotourism is seen as a vital piece in this jigsaw. The recreational use of protected areas by both nationals and foreign visitors creates employment for the local people and increases revenue for the community. It also, importantly, fosters an increased pride in local resources, and engenders the feeling that Borneo's forests and wildlife are very special and worth preserving, not only for commercial reasons, but also for intrinsic, aesthetic and spiritual ones.

This is not to say that ecotourism is a panacea for Borneo's environmental difficulties. It is not. However, there is every reason to believe that ecotourism has a vital role to play in the conservation of the island's biological riches.

PREVIOUS PAGE: *As the morning mists clear, there is a tingle of anticipation at the start of an early boat trip along the Menanggol River in Sabah. The diversity of life all around is bewildering.*

OPPOSITE: *More people visit Kinabalu Park than any other national park in Borneo. A good network of trails offers easy access to the montane forests, and many of these follow the course of picturesque streams.*

TOP WILDLIFE-WATCHING LOCATIONS

Borneo may not have the reputation and glamorous image of other top wildlife destinations around the world, but it offers the wildlife tourist a wealth of opportunities to experience the thrill of the island's forests and the remarkable species that live there.

It is not surprising that the majority of tourists perhaps associate Borneo with one animal, the Orang-utan: its appeal and popularity are clearly evident during any visit to a rehabilitation centre such as Sepilok. However, as the pages of this book testify, Borneo's wildlife riches are so much more numerous and diverse, and there are now an established series of parks and reserves around the island that cater for visitors at all levels.

Sabah

Without question, Sabah has some of the richest, most diverse and best developed parks and reserves in Borneo. This, coupled with relatively easy access, good infrastructure and quality tourist facilities, makes Sabah the obvious first choice for visitors. Sites such as Mount Kinabalu , Danum Valley and Lower Kinabatangan are world renowned, and offer an easy window for those wishing to experience Borneo's natural wonders.

Lower Kinabatangan Wildlife Sanctuary

The Kinabatangan River originates on the steep forested slopes of south-central Sabah, and meanders and snakes its way through the interior and coastal lowlands for 560km (350 miles), until it reaches the Sulu Sea. It is Sabah's longest river, and in its lower reaches forms a flood-plain ecosystem of almost unparalleled richness. There are tracts of riparian forest, stranded ox-bow lakes, nipa swamp and mangroves, all of which support the most diverse concentrations of wildlife in Sabah, including Orang-utans, Proboscis Monkeys, Bornean Pygmy Elephants and a vast array of birds, reptiles and amphibians.

This lower basin covers an area of nearly 4000square km (1500 square miles), some 26,000 hectares (64,250 acres), of which constitutes the Kinabatangan Wildlife Sanctuary. However, this is far from being a pristine wilderness. Perhaps as much as 90 per cent of the dipterocarp forest in the lower Kinabatangan has already been cleared to make way for cash crops, in particular palm-oil plantations. This has obviously seriously fragmented the forest, and has also adversely altered drainage patterns. In some years, around 80 per cent of the sanctuary can be under water after major floods, which leaves little or no higher ground for wildlife to seek refuge. Consequently, species such as the Bornean Pygmy Elephant are forced to move out into plantations, which typically brings them into direct confrontation with people.

To try and find solutions to alleviate these conflicts, and to address more far-reaching conservation and biodiversity issues, the Kinabatangan floodplain is now one of many key areas in the 'Partners for Wetland' initiative, a collaborative effort between WWF, the oil palm and other industries, the Sabah government and other agencies, all of whom are major stakeholders. The vision is to create a 'Kinabatangan Corridor for Life', where natural forests along the river are maintained

ABOVE: *A local fisherman casts his nets on the Kinabatangan River.*

OPPOSITE: *The Buffy Fish Owl (Ketupa ketupa) is often seen along the Kinabatangan River near Sukau.*

intact, and are re-established where fragmented; to connect the coastal mangrove swamps with dry land forests upriver; and where people, wildlife, ecotourism and local forest industries can thrive and help support one another.

Historically, the banks of the Kinabatangan River have been relatively sparsely populated, but the river itself has been a vital lifeline and highway to transport forest produce from the interior to the coast. In the early 19th century, huge quantities of wild bees' wax and edible birds' nests, for example, came down the river, a high proportion of the latter coming from the Gomangtong Caves, down the Menanngol River to the village of Sukau, and on down the Kinabatangan to Sandakan.

Sukau, about 80km (50 miles) upriver from the coast, is now the centre for wildlife tourism. Here, a number of comfortable and sympathetically constructed lodges are situated along the banks of the main river, close to the confluence with the smaller Menanggol River. The wildlife experiences this locality has to offer are amongst the most memorable in Borneo. The majority of watching is done from boats, and one of the reasons the experience is so good is that most of the wildlife is remarkably tolerant of people in boats, a consequence of the long history of river use.

The best way to reach Sukau is by boat from Sandakan (although it is also easily accessible by road). The boat journey takes around three hours, initially through vast tracts of mangrove and nipa swamp, where Oriental Short-clawed Otters live, and later through riparian forest, with hornbills flying overhead and Estuarine Crocodiles stalking the margins.

Boat journeys up the Menanggol River are particularly intimate as the river narrows and forest encroaches. Passing under overhanging boughs and skirting fallen trees, it is possible to peer into the tangled vegetation at the margins where Water Monitors bask on half-sunken trunks, and Mangrove Snakes, young Reticulated Pythons and Wagler's Pit Vipers lie concealed and motionless. There are also troops of Proboscis Monkeys (this is perhaps the best place there is to see these animals), macaques, langurs and even the occasional Orang-utan and Bornean Gibbon.

Sepilok Forest Reserve and Orang-utan Sanctuary

Opened in 1964, the Sepilok Orang-utan Sanctuary is renowned the world over for its work in rehabilitating orphaned Orang-utans. Over 250 individuals have been successfully returned to their forest home, some even breeding with established wild Orang-utans. Visitors can enjoy close encounters with these charismatic apes at the twice-daily feeding sessions in the forest, where individuals not fully capable of self-sufficiency return for a free meal.

However, set amongst 43 square km (17 square miles) of primary lowland rainforest, the reserve has much more to offer besides. Boardwalks through the forest are excellent places to wander at leisure – bird-watching is very good, and there is also a variety of snakes and frogs to look out for.

There are several lodges next to the centre's gates, although its close proximity to Sandakan makes staying on the doorstep unnecessary.

LEFT: *The canopy walkway at Danum Valley provides visitors with a bird's-eye view of the tree tops.*

Turtle Islands Park: Selingan Island

Part of the Turtle Islands Marine Park, Selingan is a tiny, sandy island in the Sulu Sea, 40km (25 miles) off the north-west coast of Sabah. Along with two similar neighbouring islands, it constitutes one of the region's major sea-turtle breeding sites. Throughout the year, and particularly between April and October, large numbers of Green Turtles and, to a lesser extent, Hawksbill Turtles, haul themselves ashore on most nights to dig nests on the beach and lay their eggs.

Each night, wardens patrol the beaches and collect all the eggs that are laid. These are then incubated in fenced enclosures free from the risk of predation. Newly hatched baby turtles are then released back into the sea. Visitors staying on the island for a night have the opportunity to watch by torchlight turtles excavating their nests and laying their clutches, and also to observe the hatchlings being released.

Danum Valley Conservation Area

The pristine lowland rainforest of Danum Valley is arguably Borneo's premier wildlife location. Situated amidst an enormous forest concession, over 400square km (154 square miles) have been set aside as a conservation area. These forests are known to harbour some of the richest concentrations of species anywhere on the island.

Borneo Rainforest Lodge lies at the heart of Danum Valley, some 80km (50 miles) off the main road from Lahad Datu. It is located on the banks of the Danum river, and facing the lodge on the opposite bank is a huge swathe of pristine forest. Within the vicinity of the lodge there is a network of well laid-out trails that follow the course of the river and forest interior. These allow easy access to most of the valley, and provide ample opportunity to discover some of the forest's amazing biodiversity.

ABOVE: *Selingan Island is one of three islands off the north-east coast of Sabah that constitute the Turtle Islands Marine Park.*

Within a stone's throw of the lodge it is possible to encounter wild Orang-utans, Red Leaf Monkeys and Bornean Gibbons. Bird-watching is also excellent; the open areas around the lodge and along the trails offer plenty of chances to see mixed feeding flocks, and if there is a fruiting tree in the vicinity, noisy Rhinoceros and Helmeted Hornbills are conspicuous.

For those wishing to experience the true atmosphere of the rainforest, a hike up the Coffin Trail to the viewpoint is recommended. If you leave the lodge at first light and walk at a good pace, it is possible to reach the viewpoint just before the sun peaks over the horizon. After a clear night, mist hangs in the valleys and clings to the crowns of trees; only the tallest emergents stand proud above the white cloak. As the sun breaks through, the canopy is briefly set on fire in a golden blaze of light beams. With gibbons calling and hornbills flying by, few more evocative experiences are imaginable.

Early mornings are also perhaps the best time to enjoy the extra dimension offered by the canopy walkway. Here, a tree-top view of the forest provides a spectacular alternative perspective and great bird-watching opportunities: various hornbills, barbets and broadbills may be seen, as well as the enigmatic and endemic Bornean Bristlehead.

After dark, night walks and vehicle rides offer a window into the secretive world of the forest's nocturnal creatures: Greater Mouse Deer, Giant Flying Squirrels and Colugo are often seen. There is also a reasonable chance of seeing both Slow Loris and Western Tarsier. Frogs, too, are common, and the resonant honk of the Bornean Horned Frog is always a feature, although tracking one down is a tough proposition.

The Maliau Basin

For those with a taste for Arthur Conan Doyle-like adventure, the Maliau Basin is just the place. Known as Sabah's 'Lost World', the Basin is a huge, saucer-shaped depression, enclosed by a high mountain rim that is located at the heart of one of the most remote and pristine parts of Sabah. The natural beauty and awe-inspiring scenery makes this one of Borneo's last great wilderness areas.

The Basin drains into the Maliau River, which becomes the Kuamut river that eventually joins the waters of the Kinabatangan. Within the Basin grows utterly untouched rainforest that changes form and composition with altitude; around the rim of the escarpment there are stands of dramatically different heath forest. The scenic highlight is the Maliau Falls, a multi-step cascade running through a gorge that exits the Basin.

The diversity of fauna and flora is stunning, including numerous endemic species that have become marooned in this 'lost world'. These include a variety of pitcher plants that flourish on the nutrient-deficient soils of the heath forest, and a dwarf orange-coloured species of *Rafflesia* that was not discovered until 1987: *Rafflesia tengku-adlini* is named after Tengku D. Z. Adlin, co-discoverer of the species, one of Sabah's foremost naturalists, Chairman of the Sabah Tourism Board and Vice-President Emeritus of WWF-Malaysia.

The Basin supports a considerable diversity of mammals, more than 80 species, including Red Leaf Monkeys; the Red-

ABOVE: *The Maliau Falls are one of the scenic highlights in Sabah's 'Lost World', one of Borneo's last great wilderness areas.*

bellied Sculptor Squirrel, a curious little rodent with outward-pointing, concave incisor teeth; over 270 species of bird, including the exceedingly rare, endemic Bulwer's Pheasant (*Lophura bulweri*); and a phenomenal diversity of amphibians and reptiles.

Not surprisingly, this biological wonderland is very difficult to reach, and is only suited to those fit enough and who don't mind being without creature comforts. Currently, a Basin 'tour' involves a five-day round trek from the nearest road access, and is all camping. Plans are underway to develop the Maliau Basin for low-impact adventure and wildlife tourism, and the sealing of the Kalabakan-Sapulut Highway will make access easier from either Tawau or Kota Kinabalu.

Tabin Wildlife Reserve

Less than two hours drive from Lahad Datu in north-east Sabah is the Tabin Wildlife Reserve. It is perhaps most notable as the last major stronghold of the Sumatran Rhinoceros on Borneo. There are also significant numbers of Bornean Pygmy Elephants and Tembadau (wild cattle) here, although these animals primarily inhabit the core area of the Reserve, which is inaccessible to visitors. The peripheral areas do support a wealth of other wildlife, however, and there is much to see

ABOVE: *Coastal dipterocarp forest begins immediately behind the beach in Bako National Park.*

even in areas where forest adjoins plantations.

Tabin Wildlife Resort is located on the edge of the reserve, and offers the visitor an excellent introduction to the area. There are numerous forest trails and watch towers, plus the opportunity for night walks and drives. The nocturnal drives can be especially rewarding, as Tabin is perhaps the best place in Borneo to see some of the island's elusive carnivores, especially cats such as the Leopard Cat, the Flat-headed Cat and, for the very fortunate, the Clouded Leopard.

Rafflesia Rainforest Reserve

Located in the Crocker Ranges, less than two hours' drive from Kota Kinabalu and near the village of Tambunan, is the Rafflesia Rainforest Reserve: this is undoubtedly the best place in Borneo to see one of the world's floral wonders: *Rafflesia*. The slightly cooler upland forests of the Crocker Ranges provide an ideal habitat for this botanical oddity: many *Rafflesia* prefer low montane areas, generally 450 to 1200m (1,475 to 3,950 feet) in altitude. The species seen in this reserve is *Rafflesia pricei*.

Remarkable not only for being the world's largest flower, *Rafflesia* is also parasitic – it grows from the stems and roots of a climbing vine related to grapes. The flower buds take months to develop to the size of a cabbage before opening into a bloom, sometimes approaching 1m (39 inches) in diameter. The bloom then produces a stench like rotting flesh, to attract flies that will pollinate it; but the display is short-lived, and after only four or five days the flower begins to wither and die.

Near the park, the Rafflesia Information Centre provides visitors with a wealth of information about the plant, and there is also an extensive network of forest trails to explore in order to see the flower itself.

Sarawak

Sarawak has an extensive network of parks and reserves, many of which are relatively easy to access. While in general they do not offer wildlife-watching experiences comparable in quality and diversity to those in Sabah (because Sarawak has suffered deforestation and hunting to a far greater degree), there are nonetheless some superb locations where the fascination and charm of the island's natural history can be appreciated.

Bako National Park

Bako offers an intoxicating mixture of stunning coastal scenery, teeming rainforests and abundant wildlife. In combination with its proximity to Kuching and easy access, this makes it arguably Sarawak's best wildlife viewing location for the first-time visitor.

Gazetted in 1957, Bako is Sarawak's oldest national park,

and is situated on a peninsula jutting into the South China Sea. Although it is relatively small, covering just 2727 hectares (74,622 acres), the Park is extremely diverse, with rocky coasts, secluded beaches, mangrove forest, lowland dipterocarp forest, peat-swamp forest and heath forest (kerangas). There is an extensive network of trails through most parts of the park, which allows the visitor to experience the best that each of these various habitats has to offer. Many of the trails through the forested areas are boardwalks.

Bako is one of the best places in Borneo to see Proboscis Monkeys, and they are regularly encountered in the mangrove forests, as well as in swamp forest and on the edge of dipterocarp forest. Telok Delima and Telok Paku are probably the two best trails to look for this monkey, and they can also be seen at times foraging on the mudflats in the mangroves at low tide. Other monkeys often seen in the park are Long-tailed Macaques and Silvered Langurs. Areas close to water are also good places to look for both Oriental Short-clawed and Hairy-nosed Otters. Other mammals that are seen on night walks from time-to-time include Colugos, Slow Loris, Pangolins and Mouse Deer.

With such a variety of habitats, the park's flora is correspondingly rich and diverse. Of particular note is the heath forest, as this is where large numbers of pitcher plants can be seen. In some places, there are large colonies and clusters of *Nepenthes ampullaria* growing on the ground, along with larger aerial species such as *Nepenthes rafflesiana* and *Nepenthes gracilis*.

The park is just 37km (23 miles) from Kuching, and is easily visited in a day, although it is much better to spend at least one night in the park. The bus from Kuching to Kampung Bako takes less than an hour, and the boat ride from the village to the park is just 20 minutes. There are lodges and self-catering hostels in the park, all located close to the park headquarters and the beach at Telok Assam.

Gunung Mulu National Park

Gunung Mulu is Sarawak's largest national park (52, 865 hectares/130,629 acres), and is dominated by three mountains: Gunung Mulu (2376m/7796 feet), Gunung Api (1750m/5742 feet) and Gunung Benarat (1585m/5200 feet), that are surrounded by rainforest. However, what lies beneath is the park's major claim to fame: one of the largest limestone cave systems in the world.

The scale of these caves is bewildering, and they include the world's largest cave passage (Deer Cave), the world's largest natural chamber (Sarawak Chamber, capable of 'housing' 47 jumbo jets), and the longest cave in South-East Asia (Clearwater Cave, 108km/67 miles in length). To date, over 300km (186 miles) of underground cave passages have been surveyed, and this is thought to represent only 30 to 40 per cent of the full extent. Visiting the mouth of Deer Cave at dusk is to witness one of the natural world's most amazing spectacles, because in excess of three million bats pour out of

BELOW: *Spectacular limestone pinnacles on Gunung Api in Mulu National Park.*

the entrance like a giant plume of black smoke.

No less than eight different major habitat types are found within the park, including dipterocarp, peat swamp, heath, montane and cloud forests, and the diversity of fauna and flora is correspondingly high. Some 75 species of mammal, over 260 species of bird, 75 species of amphibian, more than 50 species of reptile, 170 species of wild orchid and 10 species of pitcher plant have been recorded. However, many of these can be a challenge to see, particularly some of the larger mammals whose populations have suffered as a consequence of hunting pressure from local tribes.

For the visitor, Mulu offers much more than simply wildlife: there is rock climbing, adventurous jungle trekking, kayaking, mountain biking and interaction with fascinating local people, including the Iban and Berawan, and the Penan, Sarawak's last nomadic tribe.

For the fit and adventurous, the trek to Gunung Api to see the breathtaking Pinnacles is a worthwhile challenge. These razor-sharp limestone peaks soar above the surrounding forest like an army of sentinels.

The park offers a variety of accommodation options, from chalets to hostels and a camping ground. For those wanting more comfort, there is also a high-quality lodge adjacent to the park on the banks of the Melinau river.

Mulu can be reached by daily flights from Miri, or by boat via Marundi or Kuala Baram. Express boats travel as far as Long Terawan on the Baram river; from there the journey continues by longboat up the Tutoh and Melinau rivers to the park.

Lambir Hills National Park

Lambir Hills is perhaps most notable for its botanical richness. The park covers 6952 hectares (17,178 acres), and is dominated by stands of mixed dipterocarp forest: one modest-sized plot (52 hectares/128 acres) is known to contain 1,175 species of tree. There are also areas of heath forest (kerangas) growing on the

LEFT: *A delightful waterfall and pool in Lambir Hills National Park.*

sandstone escarpment, where pitcher plants flourish.

Mammals known to inhabit the park include Long-tailed Macaques, Leaf Monkeys, various bats, and muntjac deer, although these can be difficult to see. The park's bird life is diverse, and over 150 species have been recorded. A tree tower on the Pantu Trail is probably the best place to bird-watch.

The park is only 30km (18 miles) from Miri, and can be readily reached by public transport. There are forest lodges and chalets within the park.

Gunung Gading National Park

Located on Sarawak's south-west coast, Gunung Gading is known as one of the few places in the state to see *Rafflesia*. The species in question is *Rafflesia tuan-mudae*, which is only found in the south-western corner of Borneo, and bears close resemblance to *Rafflesia arnoldi,* found in Sumatra. Large blooms can measure over 70cm (27 inches) in diameter.

There is a network of boardwalks through the accessible areas of forest where the Rafflesia grow. If there are blooms deeper into the forest, park staff can sometimes escort visitors. Before travelling, it is advisable to check with the park's department to see whether there are in fact any flowers in bloom.

Gunung Gading is about two hours by road from Kuching. Accommodation within the park is basic and limited, but there are a few hostels in nearby Lundu Pandan and Siar.

Brunei

Less well-known than its larger neighbours, Brunei has only recently (within the last decade) begun to develop its tourism and ecotourism potential. Because of wealth generated from its oil and gas reserves, Brunei has not needed to exploit its forests, and logging has been only a minor issue. This, combined with a small

ABOVE: *The forests of Gunung Gading National Park are a refuge for* Rafflesia tuan-mudae, *the large blooms of which can measure over 70cm (27 inches) in diameter.*

population and reduced pressure on the environment, mean around 75 per cent of the State's forests remain intact. Correspondingly, Brunei still has natural areas of significance and parks where an excellent appreciation of wildlife can be gained. Relatively good infrastructure and accommodation makes travelling here easy.

Ulu Temburong National Park
Ulu Temburong National Park (formerly the Batu Apoi Forest Reserve) is located in the easternmost corner of Brunei. It is primarily lowland dipterocarp forest dominated by giants of the genera *Shorea, Dryobalanops* and *Dipterocarpus,* and falls within the boundaries of the 'Heart of Borneo' (see pages 142-147). From the park headquarters, an extensive network of boardwalks leads to the surrounding forests.

One of the park's highlights is an impressive canopy tower and walkway, suspended 50m (164 feet) above the forest floor. Tiger orchids and other epiphytes can be seen clinging to nearby branches, and birds such as Bushy Crested Hornbills and Black-and-Yellow Broadbills are common. Bornean Gibbons are generally heard each morning.

Common reptiles include the strikingly coloured Wagler's Pit Viper, the Five-lined Flying Lizard (*Draco* sp.) and the Bent-toed Gecko (*Gonydactylus* sp.). Amphibian life is rich and varied, too: Kuhl's Creek Frog, Smooth Guardian Frog, Painted Tree Frog and Wallace's Flying Frog are regularly seen species. Over 400 species of butterfly have been seen in the park, including Rajah Brooke's Birdwing.

Ulu Temburong is accessible only by boat. From the capital of Bandar Seri, Begawan water taxis take about one hour to reach the town of Bangar; en route Proboscis Monkeys may be seen in mangroves flanking the Limbang river. From Bangar it is a short bus ride to Batang Duri, where Temuai longboats can be taken up the Temburong river to the park. Accommodation is available at the park headquarters.

Kalimantan
Access to the wildlife hotspots of Kalimantan is generally more difficult than visiting locations in other parts of Borneo. This is because getting to Kalimantan itself is less straightforward than getting to Malaysian Borneo (Sarawak and Sabah) or Brunei, and also because infrastructure within Kalimantan is much less developed and travel can be more time-consuming.

Tanjung Puting National Park

Lying just inland from the south coast of Central Kalimantan, Tanjung Puting National Park sits on a peninsula surrounded by the Java Sea. The peninsula is low lying, and nowhere does its elevation rise above 30m (100 feet).

The park, which was gazetted in 1982, officially covers 3,040square km (1174 square feet) of lowland dipterocarp and peat swamp forest, with nipa palm and mangroves around the coast. It is the largest protected forest in Central Kalimantan, and one of the largest protected areas of tropical heath forest and peat swamp forest in South-East Asia. It is also one of the most important remaining wild Orang-utan areas in Borneo.

The park initially gained renown as the site for the long-term Orang-utan research carried out by Dr Biruté Galdikas, based at Camp Leakey. From informal beginnings in 1971, this later became one of the island's foremost rehabilitation centres. Its success at releasing rehabilitated Orang-utans brought its problems, however, as tourist numbers increased dramatically. Ironically, this influx undermined the rehabilitation process and increased the risk of introducing serious human diseases to the rehabilitated Orang-utans, who then could potentially transmit disease to the wild population. In 1995, new regulations in Kalimantan prohibited the reintroduction of Orang-utans into areas currently supporting wild populations, and the releases into Tanjung Puting stopped. The park nonetheless supports a thriving population of wild and previously released animals, and is considered to have a population of around 5,000 Orang-utans.

Tanjung Puting supports much more besides Orang-utans, and there are good populations of Proboscis Monkeys, Agile Gibbons (*Hylobates agilis*) and Silvered Langurs. Clouded Leopards, various civets, Sun Bears, and wild cattle or Banteng (Tembadau) have also been recorded, as have several species of hornbill and a great diversity of bird life, especially waterfowl, egrets, herons and storks.

Access is via the towns of Pangkalan Bun (the nearest airport) and Kumai, then by boat to Tanjung Harapan (two-and-a-half hours), where there is accommodation (Rimba Lodge or Eco Lodge). The park and Camp Leakey are then a further two hours by boat along the blackwater Sekonyer river.

Gunung Palung National Park

Located on and around Mount Palung and Mount Panti in West Kalimantan (on the south-west coast of Borneo), Gunung Palung National Park covers 90,000 hectares (222,390 acres), and boasts a diversity of habitats and flora to rival virtually anywhere in Borneo. Gunung Palung itself is a horse-shoe-shaped peak (1100m/3609 feet) that rises from flat, swampy lowlands, producing an island of dry dipterocarp forest with unusual montane forest above. The low-lying areas encompass beaches and mangrove forest, along with peat forest and freshwater swamp forest.

There is a healthy population of wild Orang-utans, and a well established and ongoing research base at Cabang Panti Research Camp on the southern side of the mountain. Other primates include Proboscis Monkeys, Agile Gibbons, Long-tailed Macaques and Red Leaf Monkeys. Bird life is particularly rich, with most of Borneo's lowland bird groups represented, and rarities include White-crowned Hornbills, Bornean Bristleheads and Bornean Peacock-Pheasants.

The park is one of the least accessible in Kalimantan, and is only suitable for those with a real spirit of adventure and lots of time at their disposal. Journeys begin at Pontianak, either by boat or plane to Ketapang, and on to Sukadana. From Sukadana it is necessary to hire a boat for the ten-hour trip to the park.

Sebangau Wildlife Sanctuary

Sebangau is one of the largest remaining peat swamp forest areas in Central Kalimantan, and harbours one of the biggest lowland populations of Orang-utans (2,500 to 4,500). It is located in an area where major threats such as forest fires and conversion to plantations are omnipresent. However, local Dayak communities have for centuries acknowledged the ecological and spiritual values of this large coastal and inland forest area, and the creation of a reserve in 2004 has done much to provide a safeguard.

WWF is working with local communities and major stakeholders in the region to develop community-based economic initiatives, and the continuing improvement of infrastructure and access for ecotourism will further strengthen the position of the reserve.

Pleihari Martapura Wildlife Reserve

This reserve covers 36,000ha (96,680 square miles), and lies some 30km (18 miles) from the coast on the extreme southern tip of Kalimantan. It also encompasses the southern and western slopes of the isolated Meratus Mountain range.

The main habitats here are fire-climax 'alang-alang' grasslands, brush-vegetation, montane forest, dipterocarp forest and swamp forest. The mountain forest is rich in orchids, with several species endemic to the Meratus Mountains. Notable mammals include six species of primate (Long-tailed Macaque, Pig-tailed Macaque, Proboscis Monkey, Red Leaf Monkey, Silver Leaf Monkey and Bornean Gibbon), as well as the Pangolin, the Sun Bear and the Clouded Leopard, while birds include the Great Argus Pheasant, the Sunda Woodpecker and the Pin-tailed Parrotfinch.

Access to the reserve is relatively straightforward from Banjarmasin, and overnight stays can be arranged in local longhouses.

Glossary

adaptive radiation A burst of evolution, whereby an ancestral form undergoes rapid diversification into many new forms, resulting in the exploitation of an array of habitats (cf. convergent evolution).

arboreal Animals that spend the majority of their lives living in trees.

carnivore Generally applied to any primarily flesh-eating organism. More specifically refers to members of the taxonomic order Carnivora.

cauliflory Where trees produce flowers and fruits directly from their trunk.

class A taxonomic category that is subordinate to phylum and superior to order, e.g. the mammals are class Mammalia in phylum Chordata (see taxonomy).

convergent evolution The independent acquisition through evolution of similar characteristics in unrelated taxonomic groupings that lead to similar ways of life, as opposed to the possession of similarities by virtue of descent from a common ancestor.

crepuscular Of twilight: the term applies to animals that are primarily active around dusk.

Diurnal Applied to animals that are primarily active during the day time (cf. nocturnal).

Dipterocarp Tree belonging to the family Dipterocarpaceae: a family of statuesque rainforest trees characterized by winged seeds.

Endemic Where a species or other taxonomic grouping is naturally restricted to a particular geographic region: such a taxon is then said to be endemic to that region. In this context, the size of the region will usually depend on the status of the taxon: thus, all other factors being equal, a family will be endemic to a larger area than a genus or a species. For instance the Proboscis Monkey is endemic to the island of Borneo as a whole, while the pitcher plant *Nepenthes rajah* is endemic to two mountains (Gunung Kinabalu and Gunung Tambuyukon) at the very north-western tip of the island (cf. indigenous and exotic).

exotic Refers to a taxonomic grouping (usually a species) that has been accidentally or deliberately introduced to a region in which it does not occur naturally (cf. indigenous).

family A taxonomic category that is subordinate to order and superior to subfamily, e.g. the mongooses, family Herpestidae (see taxonomy).

frugivore Applied to an animal that feeds primarily on fruit.

genus (plural genera) A taxonomic category that is subordinate to subfamily and superior to species, e.g. the gibbons, genus *Hylobates* (see taxonomy).

Gunung Mount or mountain in Malay.

indigenous Applies to species or other taxonomic groupings that occur naturally in a specified area or region and have, therefore, not been introduced either deliberately or accidentally by man. This term is synonymous with native (cf. endemic and exotic).

kerangas Term used in Borneo to describe heath forest. Derived from the Iban dialect.

niche The functional position or role of an organism (usually applied to a species) within its community and environment, defined in all aspects of its lifestyle, e.g. food, competitors, predators and other resource requirements. Also referred to as ecological niche.

nocturnal Applied to animals that are primarily active during the night (cf. diurnal and cathemeral).

omnivore Applied to an animal with a varied diet that feeds on both flesh and vegetation.

order A taxonomic category that is subordinate to class and superior to family, e.g. the rodents – order Rodentia (see taxonomy).

prosimian Literally meaning 'before the monkeys': used as a collective term referring to the relatively primitive primates belonging to the suborder Strepsirhini (formerly Prosimii) that includes the lemurs, galagos, pottos and lorises.

species A taxonomic category that is subordinate to genus and superior to subspecies e.g. the Orang-utan (*Pongo pygmaeus*). This is the fundamental unit of taxonomy and is broadly defined as a population of organisms with like morphology that are able to interbreed and produce viable offspring, i.e. they have compatible gametes and share a common fertilization technique (see taxonomy).

speciation The process by which new species arise by evolution. It is widely accepted that this occurs when a single species population becomes divided, and then different selection pressures acting on each new population cause them to diverge.

subspecies A taxonomic category that is subordinate to species and denotes a recognizable sub-population within a single species that typically has a distinct geographical range, e.g. the Asian Elephant (*Elephas maximus*) is divided into three subspecies: *E. m. maximus* from Sri Lanka, *E. m. indicus* from the mainland Indian Subcontinent and South-East Asia, and *E. m. sumatrensis* from Sumatra. The newly recognized type on Borneo, *Elephas maximus borneensis*, is thought to represent a fourth subspecies. Subspecies is interchangeable with the term 'race' (see taxonomy).

taxonomy The science of classifying organisms. In this classification system, organisms that share common features are grouped together and are, therefore, thought to share a common ancestry. Each individual is thus a member of a series of ever-broader categories (individual – species – genus – family – order – class – phylum – kingdom), and each of these categories can be further divided where convenient and appropriate (e.g. subspecies, subfamily, superfamily or infraorder).

terrestrial Refers to animals that spend the majority of their lives living on the ground.

Wildlife Guides & Reference Volumes

Bennett, Elizabeth L. *The Natural History of Orang-Utan* Natural History Publications 1998 (Borneo).

Bennett, Elizabeth L. & Gombek, Francis *Proboscis Monkeys of Borneo* Natural History Publications 1993 (Borneo).

Bragg, Philip E. *The Phasmids of Borneo* Natural History Publications 2001 (Borneo).

Clarke, Charles *Nepenthes of Borneo* Natural History Publications 1997 (Borneo).

Das, Indraneil *Lizards of Borneo: A Pocket Guide* Natural History Publications 2004 (Borneo).

Davidson, G.W.H. & Chew Yen Fook *Photographic Guide to the Birds of Borneo* New Holland 2000

Hazebroek, Hans P., Tengku Zainal Adlin & Waidi Sinun *Maliau Basin: Sabah's Lost World* Natural History Publications 2004 (Borneo).

Hutton, Wendy & Prudente, Cede *Kinabatangan: Sabah Colour Guide* Natural History Publications 2004 (Borneo).

Inger, Robert & Stuebing, Robert *A Field Guide to the Frogs of Borneo (2ⁿᵈ ed.)* Natural History Publications 2005 (Borneo).

Inger, Robert & Tan Fui Lian *The Natural History of Amphibians and Reptiles in Sabah* Natural History Publications 1996 (Borneo).

MacKinnon, John & Phillipps, Karen *A Field Guide to the Birds of Borneo, Sumatra, Java & Bali* Oxford University Press 1993. Out of Print.

Malkmus, R., Manthey, U., Vogel, G., Hoffman, P., and Kosuch, J. *The Amphibians and Reptiles of Mount Kinabalu* Koeltz Scientific Books 2002 (Germany).

Nais, Jamili *Rafflesia of the World* Natural History Publications 2001 (Borneo).

Oakley, S. & Pilcher, N. & Wood, E. *Seas at the Millennium, An Environmental Evaluation: Borneo* C.R.C Sheppard ed. Pergamon Press 2000 (Amsterdam)

Orr, A.G. *A Guide to the Dragonflies of Borneo* Natural History Publications 2003 (Borneo).

Otsuka, Kazuhisa *A Field Guide to the Butterflies of Borneo and South East Asia* Hornbill Books 2001 (Kota Kinabalu).

Payne, Junaidi & Cubitt, Gerald & Lau, Dennis & Langub, Jayl *This is Borneo* New Holland 2005

Payne, Junaidi & Francis, Charles *A Field Guide to the Mammals of Borneo* The Sabah Society & WWF (5th ed.) 2005.

Phillipps, Anthea & Liew, Francis

Globetrotter Visitor's Guide to Kinabalu Park New Holland 2000.

Smythies, B.E. & Davidson, G.W.H. *The Birds of Borneo* (4th ed.) 2001.

Stuebing, Robert & Inger, Robert *A Field Guide to the Snakes of Borneo* Natural History Publications 1999 (Borneo).

Wong, K.M., & Phillipps, A. *Kinabalu, Summit of Borneo (eds, 2nd ed.)* The Sabah Society and Sabah Parks 1996 (Kota Kinabalu).

General Travel Guides

The following guides are recommended for their accessible style and all-round coverage of Borneo's areas of interest:

Adventure Guide to East Malaysia (Sarawak & Sabah) & Brunei. Wendy Hutton (ed) 1997, Periplus Editions

Adventure Guide to Peninsula Malaysia (West) Wendy Hutton (ed) 1997, Periplus Editions

Insight Pocket Guide: Sabah Wendy Hutton 2001, ABA Publications

Adventure Guide to Kalimantan (Indonesian Borneo) Kal Muller 1996, Periplus Editions

There is also a considerable choice of guides from a variety of leading travel publishers:

Globetrotter Guide to Malaysia

Blue Guide to Malaysia and Singapore

Nelles Guide: Malaysia, Singapore & Brunei

Lonely Planet: Malaysia, Singapore & Brunei

Rough Guide: Malaysia, Singapore & Brunei

Insight Guide: Malaysia

Footprint Guide: Malaysia

The above guides all cover peninsula Malaysia plus Sarawak and Sabah (East Malaysia) on Borneo. The above series also have guides to Indonesia that include sections on Kalimantan.

Useful Contacts and Addresses

Brunei Tourism Board
Ministry of Industry and Primary Resources,
Jalan Menteri Besar
BB2910 Brunei Darussalam
Tel:+673 238 28 22 / +673 238 28 32
Fax: +673 238 28 24
E-mail: info@tourismbrunei.com

Indonesian Culture and Tourism Board
Sapta Pesona Building 21st floor
Jalan Medan Merdeka Barat 17
Jakarta 10110
INDONESIA
Tel: +62-21-3838717, Fax : +62-21-3452006
E-mail: pusdatin@budpar.go.id

Sabah Tourism Promotion Corporation
Ministry of Tourism Development,
Environment, Science and Technology Sabah
51, Jalan Gaya
88000 Kota Kinabalu
Sabah, Malaysia
Tel: +6088 21212, Fax: +6088 212075
Email: info@sabahtourism.com

Sarawak Tourism Board
6th & 7th Floor, Bangunan Yayasan Sarawak
Jalan Masjid, 93400 Kuching,
Sarawak, Malaysia.
Tel: +6082 423600, Fax: +6082 416700
Email: stb@sarawaktourism.com

TRAFFIC South East Asia: Regional Office
Unit 9-3A, 3rd Floor
Jalan SS23/11, Taman SEA
47400 Petaling Jaya
Selangor, Malaysia
tsea@po.jaring.my
www.traffic.org

ECOTOURISM

Natural Selection Photo Tours, Papyrus Tours
Topham Farm, Topham Ferry Lane
Sykehouse, Goole, East Yorks,
DN14 9BQ, UK
www.naturalselectionphototours.co.uk

North Borneo Safaris
Lot 4, 1st Floor Block 22
Bandar Indah Mile 4, 90000
Sandakan, Sabah, Malaysia
www.sabahtravelguide.com/photosafari

See also www.wildasia.net, an ecotourism site that promotes the exploration, documentation and conservation of natural areas in Asia.

THE HEART OF BORNEO

The Heart of Borneo is a major global initiative for WWF in co-operation with the local communities and governments of Borneo, the general public anywhere in the world, NGOs and other organizations. It is a case of now or never, but it will still require sustained effort over many years. You can support this work through the following offices:

WWF-Malaysia
49, Jalan SS23/15, Taman SEA
47400 Petaling Jaya, Selangor, Malaysia
Tel: +60 3 7803 3772, Fax: +60 3 7803 5157
Email: wwfmal@wwf.org.my
Website: www.wwfmalaysia.org

WWF-Indonesia
Kantor Taman A9, Unit A-1
Jalan Mega Kuningan
Jakarta 12950, Indonesia
Tel: +62 21 576 1070, Fax: +62 21 576 1080
Email: wwf-indonesia@wwf.or.id
Website: www.wwf.or.id

WWF International
Avenue du Mont-Blanc
CH-1196, Gland VD, Switzerland
Tel: + 41 22 364 9111, Fax: +41 22 364 5358
Website: www.panda.org

WWF-Denmark
Ryesgade 3 F
2200 Copenhagen N., Denmark
Tel: +45 35 36 3635, Fax: +45 35 24 7868
Website: www.wwf.dk

WWF-Germany
Rebstocker Str.55
60326 Frankfurt/Main, Germany
Tel: +49 69 79 1440, Fax: +49 69 61 7221
Website: www.wwf.de

WWF-Netherlands
Boulevard 12
3707 BM Zeist
Postbu 7
3700 AA Zeist, The Netherlands
Tel: +31 30 6937 333, Fax: +31 30 6912 064
Website: www.wnf.nl

WWF-Sweden
Ulriksdals Slott
170 81 Solna, Sweden
Tel: +46 8 624 7400, Fax: +46 8 85 1329
Website: www.wwf.se

WWF-Switzerland
Hohlstrasse 110
Postfach
8010 Zurich, Switzerland
Tel: + 41 1 297 2121, Fax: +41 1 297 2100
Website: www.wwf.ch

WWF-UK
Panda House
Weyside Park
Godalming, Surrey GU7 1XR, UK
Tel: +44 1483 426 444, Fax: +44 1483 426 409
Website: www.wwf-uk.org

WWF-USA
1250 24th St. N.W
Washington, D.C. 20037-1193, USA
Tel: +1 202 293 4800, Fax: +1 202 293 9211
Website: www.worldwildlife.org

INDEX